Sacred Ceremonies:

Rituals for the Soul

Sacred Ceremonies:

Rituals For the Soul

A Personal Resource For Celebrating Life

By

Cathyann Fisher

Amethyst & Emerald Publishing

Santa Clara, CA

Excerpts from **Spirit Medicine** are used with permission of Sterling Publishing Co., Inc., 387 Park Ave. S., NY, NY 10016 from Spirit Medicine by Wolf Moondance, c 1995 by Wolf Moondance.

Excerpts from **Celebration of Customs and Rituals** by Robert Ingpen and Phillip Wilkinson, Copyright (c) 1994 by Dragon's World Ltd. are reprinted by permission of Facts On File, Inc.

Excerpts from **Mandala** by Jose and Miriam Arguelles, Copyright 1972 are reprinted by arrangement by Shambala Publications, Inc.

Excerpts from **Casting the Circle: A Women's Book of Ritual** by Diane Stein. Copyright 1990 Published by The Crossing Press: Freedom, CA.

Excerpts from **Women's Medicine Ways: Cross-Cultural Rites of Passage** by Marcia Stark. Copyright 1993 Published by The Crossing Press: Freedom, CA.

Excerpts from **Body, The Ultimate Symbol** by Olivia Vlahos are reprinted by permission of Olivia Vlahos, who writes books and articles which apply the findings of anthropology to matters of current concern.

ISBN 1-891391-01-1

Library of Congress Card Number 98-87961

Acknowledgements

The Santa Clara Public Library

Rachel & Joshua for their enthusiasm and support
with another one of Mom's adventures

Tamera & Tess for introducing me to the world of
ritual and ceremony, and to the various members of
our group who grew together as goddesses

Zan, who encourages me to fly on past the sunset
into the stars

Foreword

Is your daily life boring? Filled with routines? What if the shower you took in the morning became a re-baptism in which you cleansed the vessel of your soul each day? What would happen if your working day began by connecting spiritually before you tackled the responsibilities at your desk? Could dreary weather become an opportunity to break out a planned ceremony of warmth and comfort? Is dinner a chore or an opportunity to replenish the body? What marks the difference between ritual and routine?

When most people hear the word ritual, images of brainwashing cults or strict religious dogma come to mind. Ritual is seen to be primitive and restricting in a world where technology and freedom prevail.

I became actively involved in the realm of ceremony and ritual when two women friends started meeting once a month to enhance their spirituality. Our religious backgrounds were varied. Our skills were minimal. Underneath our skins, our spiritual expression breathed a sigh of relief.

Trips to metaphysical bookstores, web pages, magazine subscriptions, lectures and workshops became treasure hunts for the spiritual keys to unlock our innermost beings. Once a month, we rotated leadership and location, opening our homes and hearts to one another. Twice a year we expanded our women's group to curious co-ed partners. Our daughters, nieces and grandchildren participated in a ceremony specially centered around girls entering womanhood – something that most women, who were present that day, had not experienced themselves.

Sacred Ceremonies is a comprehensive resource of cultural and sacred rituals for an individual, family, group or community. This book does not limit itself to any particular tradition, instead, it explores possibilities from many sources.

- Cathyann Fisher

Table of Contents

"All God's creations have power. To use power in Hetep (peace and harmony) you must accept yourself - your past, your culture and its contributions. Then you can bring them to the world, to help you learn the world. If you don't, you will always be searching, trying to fill up that hole in your soul, made when you ignored who you are."   - Sule Greg Wilson

The Importance of Ritual

The Meaning of Ritual

"In man ritual is rooted in the intuitional realm of vision - his deeper nature. It is applied at those junctures of life when the order of things must be clearly seen, and the splendor of the greater Light allowed to shine through the purified passages of being." 1

Ritual is the means by which men and women gain spiritual connection. Ritual knowledge transforms the participant during life transitions and causes measurable changes in their life. Communal rituals require the presence of the entire community, thereby building a unified connection. Family ritual involves a sub-community of family members, unified in purpose by tradition. From the communal and family rituals come the individual rituals. Individual rituals are interdependent, in other words, the individual participating in the ritual affects those around him by his personal connection to the spirit world. When the particular individual performs these rites, he or she does so for the sake of the community. For example, if a rain dance or medicine ritual is not performed correctly, then the entire community suffers.

"Ritual has traditionally been the means of maintaining human activity in conscious accordance with the laws of nature. The purpose of ritual is to make man a more conscious agent of cosmic forces. A ritual initiates the organism into an expanded and intensified participation in the workings of the universe." 2

Ritual requires space and time without interruption. This time, space and spiritual connection creates awareness. By taking part in a ritual, the participant honors a duty to their higher self. They no longer move senselessly through the day, closed off in their own world. The disconnected person can return to the spiritual through ritual, and reconnect themselves to community. This emphasis on community is essential. The purpose of ritual is not to emphasize self-improvement, although the higher self is nourished through the process. All ritual is a communal event to main-

---

[1.] Arguelles, Jose & Miriam *Mandala* page 82

[2.] Arguelles, Jose & Miriam *Mandala* page 83

tain a connection with spirit. When the spirit world is called to participate in the lives of humans, the two worlds join in purpose, an unexpected result can occur, and the gaps between our human limitations are filled.

For years, the prejudiced modern world has held traditional wisdom at bay. The West has considered ritual to be evil, primitive, superstitious, or quaint. Traditional ceremonies and rituals have been trivialized as exotic novelties to be passively observed. Symbolic ritual elements become mere decorative art to be hung on walls, placed in display cabinets, or hung from the rear view mirror of a car. The difference between art and craft is the breath of life. Every part of ritual contains the artistic uniqueness of this essence.

Malidoma Patrice Some speaks of the spiritual power invoked through ritual, in his book *Ritual: Power, Healing and Community.*

"The power that is felt, entertained, nourished and kept alive from within through ritual has a much different effect on a person who may be a victim of overt power. This kind of power is what many people in the West seek avidly, and, in most cases, unsuccessfully. It is spiritual power, a power that is invisible, and yet whose presence can be felt in terms of gentleness, love and compassion.

A person who lives in constant touch with the invisible realm of incomparable power is always in a good temperament and very understanding of people and situations. He does not fall prey to retaliatory invitations and does not experience wide swings in mood... Whatever happens in a ritual space, some kind of power is released if given a freedom in which to live. This is the only way those who participate in the ritual can continue to benefit from the power. The forces aroused in the ritual function like a power plant into which every individual is hooked. When one leaves the ritual space, the power of the ritual goes wherever the person goes. Only in ritual can the "here" follow you to the "there."...A sacred life is a ritualized life, that is, one that draws constantly from the realm of the spiritual to handle even the smallest situation.3

---

3. Some, Malidoma Patrice *Ritual: Power, Healing and Community* page 60

Elements of Ritual

Elements in the Sacred Space of Ritual

―――――――――――――――――――《◆》―――――――――――――

Nearly all rituals have a thread of symbolic similarity. Rituals must be repeated and slightly scripted so that each participant has a sense of what is expected of them. Ritual elements each have a distinctive and characteristic function within the ceremony. Ignoring an element of a ritual may cause confusion and conflict, or it may diminish the sacredness of the ceremony.

Preparation (Purification): All participants of a ritual should prepare themselves before the ceremony begins. Such preparations may include fasting, decorating the body with oils or paints, costume design, bathing, smudging or prayers. Meditation or other forms of releasing the outside world, help the participant to become fully present and available for the ritual.

Invocation: To begin a ritual without inviting the Spirit means that you are on your own. The tradition of the ritual will determine which "spirits" are invited. Goddesses, "the directions," power animals, ancestors or deities can be invited to participate and add spiritual power to ritual. Invocation ensures a modified outcome or a spiritual transformation.

Repetition: Particular structures within a ritual remain the same: the passing of sacrament, specific prayers, dance steps, time of the year, duration, movements, or physical materials. If these structures are not followed exactly, in certain ceremonies, then the ritual fails. Repetition within a ritual is a comfort, something that can be counted on amidst the constant chaos of change. Repetition enables discipline, it reflects the wholeness of perfection in action.

Guided Meditation: Many modern rituals or ceremonies contain guided meditation. This powerful tool allows individuals to gain personal experience and insightful revelation on the specific topic of the ritual. This individual experience is shared, in safety and love, with the rest of the group. Not only does the individual benefit from the experience, but the group, as a whole, becomes closer through the vulnerability of openness and honesty.

Symbolic Event: At the heart of ritual is symbolism. This is where the division between the spirit and human world is lessened. The gap between the two worlds is minimal. Humans participate in the power of the spirit world with the help of the deities invited within the ritual. The dancer becomes the deity, the priest or priestess becomes the representative of the god or goddess, and the participants have a sacred opportunity to communicate directly with the spirit world.

Opening and Closing: Ritual space is opened by the invocation of spirit. When the ceremony is complete, the participation of the spirit is thanked and released. Upon releasing the presence of the spirit, we are saying that we have completed what was initiated. Both spirit and participant return to their normal lives. The opening and closing are important sections of the ceremony. If the ritual is not formally closed, then the spirit has to continue to hang around because it has been forgotten. The spirit will tend to remind us that we have forgotten it through accidents and conflict. This would be the equivalent to calling a friend on the telephone, putting the phone down and going about your business without ever saying goodbye and hanging up.

Reflection: I would add this sacred quiet aspect of ritual to our awareness. It is not enough to have participated fully in any ritual or ceremony, but that our lives become whole through the experience. To walk away from the event, as if you have just watched an interesting movie, would do a grave injustice to participation in the ritual. Reflection enables the participant to cement the event into their consciousness, and to bond with the feeling of community and sacred power.

The Directions

The purpose of casting a circle is to create a protected and sacred space. This is often accomplished by an invocation to the four directions: North, South, East, and West. Other traditional directions: Above, Below, Within or Mother Earth, Father Sky, and Center may also be included. The tradition (Native American, Celtic, Tribal, Wiccan or Goddess) will determine which aspects to be included within the ritual. The four directions themselves and their corresponding associations are invited to the circle during the invocation.

There are various sources to determine the correspondences for each direction. The traditions vary, therefore, only a few correspondences are listed here. The focus of the ritual will determine the choice of one type of tradition over another.[4]

East	South	West	North
intellect	innocence	reflection	strength
morning	grounding	evening	spirit
fire	earth	water	wind/air
birds	animals	plants	minerals
spring	summer	autumn	winter
wisdom	home	dreams	prayer
birth	growth	aging	death
beginning	fulfillment	flowing	ending
topaz	emerald	amethyst	quartz
Gaia	Ishtar	Yemaya	Spider Woman
Persephone	Ashtoreth	Innana	Demeter
Candlemas	Beltane	Lammas	Yule
Spring Equinox	Summer Solstice	Fall Equinox	Winter Solstice

---

[4] Stein, Diane *The Women's Spirituality Book* page 70
Arrien, Angeles *The Four-Fold Way* pages 132 - 133
Ywahoo, Dhani *Voices of Our Ancestors* pages 249 - 252

Crystals

Meditating with crystals is the practice of opening a door to healing. Crystals do not do *for* you, but rather amplify who you already are. By freeing the mind of anger, pain and doubt we are able to see our own internal crystal quality, thereby unlocking the gem of wisdom within.

When meditating with crystals, look at their shape and movement of atomic structure. The atomic structure of a crystal is similar to the atoms of consciousness moving within us, as well as those moving throughout the universe. The shape and dimensions of crystal structures reflect an inner living form. Like us, the form expresses dimensions of decision and cycles. Crystals carry a story of formation. Within their form is a story of journey, of heating and cooling, and of tension and release.

The form of a crystal can be utilized as a guide to our minds. A quartz crystal contains six sides. These sides can be formed in many different combinations of directions, creating variations of facets, according to the energy available while forming the crystal. This energy is never lost. The quality of a crystal is contained in its ability to refract the greatest amount of light. Human quality is measured by the expression of Inner Light. The crystal seeks to be polished and refined. Human beings seek to realize their full potential.

Each crystal is a part of a greater whole, it is part of a family of crystals. When we meditate with one crystal we connect to a larger collective body of information, thereby becoming aware of our own connection to something greater than ourselves.5

The following chart is a sample of crystals and their associated qualities and directions. These associated qualities are based upon various traditions.

---

5. Ywahoo, Dhani *Voices of Our Ancestors* pages 31, 249 - 263

Crystal	Associated Direction	Associated Qualities
Quartz	North	Seed of life, will energy, action, intention, being
Diamond	North	Will energy, action, being
Topaz	East	Building intelligence, transformation, the process of remembering
Orange Jasper	Southeast	Manifestation of beauteous form, solar energy
Emerald, Bloodstone	South	Place of perfect balance, receptivity, wisdom of particulars and science, drawing swelling & poisons from the body
Rose Quartz	Northeast	Reawaken a heart stilled by grief, refreshing and renewing to cells of the body, sense of spiritual devotion, opens the door of awareness
Red Corral	Northeast	Draws heat, used for body trauma
Amethyst	West	Transformation, transmutation
Lapis, Turquoise	Northwest	The day & night of our consciousness
Pearl		Luminescent planetary mind
Ruby, Garnet	Southwest	Understanding solar energy, deep belief, understanding through experience
Fire Opal		Individuated mind awake in the solar stream
Tourmaline	South	Awakened mindfulness of relationships
Amber		Accumulated solar essence of living plants
Azurite		Energy of reconciliation
Aconite		Completion of cycle, systems unwinding, return to emptiness

Power Animals

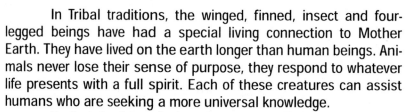

In Tribal traditions, the winged, finned, insect and four-legged beings have had a special living connection to Mother Earth. They have lived on the earth longer than human beings. Animals never lose their sense of purpose, they respond to whatever life presents with a full spirit. Each of these creatures can assist humans who are seeking a more universal knowledge.

During the "time before time" or the Creation Time, animals and humans communicated with one another. Before the time of "the fall," animals and humans spoke the same language in Paradise. Many folk or fairy tales speak of animal companions who traveled with a hero or heroine on his or her journey. Ancient peoples relied on their animals not only for food, but also to act as messengers, to warn of danger, fluctuations in weather and seasonal changes.

What is called "power" in the term "power animal" is an implied "spiritual power," not a physical size or strength. The spiritual power of this animal is that of inherent knowledge and the wisdom of living in accordance with the laws of nature; in other words, in harmony and balance with their environment. During meditation, a power animal willingly shares this wisdom with its human companion. Shaman believe that a particular animal spirit seeks out its human companion because there is a mutual need between them, and that both are destined to work together.[6]

[6.] Cowan, Tom *Shamanism As a Spiritual Practice for Daily Life* pages 23 - 28
Eagle Man, Ed McGaa *Mother Earth Spirituality* pages 161 - 175

Power animals can be called in various ways. Popular methods include vision quests, meditation, dreaming, imagery, and drumming. While communicating with a power animal, let go of any preconceived notions about what this animal has to say to you.

There are various sources to determine the attributes for each power animal. As you work with gathering the symbolic meaning and spiritual power of each animal, study the character of the particular animal in Nature. Study its way of behaving, physical attributes, and living conditions. The meaning of each power animal may vary between different people from different cultures, therefore, only a few power animal interpretations are listed here. These interpretations are only guidelines.7

Winged Ones

Red Hawk: associated with the rising dawn of the East. It is fearless, aggressive, swift moving, a messenger, keen-eyed, and observant. The hawk seldom has to worry about its next meal. It has the freedom and perspective of height. It can spend much of its time circling, studying and contemplating.

Snowy Owl: associated with the North Wind. It is a swift, silent hunter of the night, a bird of warning, and a bird of wisdom. It has a special vision of truth and revelation. It faces the elements, knows endurance and courage. It has a clean spirit and a pure heart.

Bald Eagle: associated with the North Wind. It is a symbol of leadership and greatest power (because it flies so high). It is close to the Great Spirit, the eyes of the one above who created all things. It has great vision and caution. It is a bird whose feathers have brushed the face of God.

Golden Eagle: associated with the West Wind (Thunderbird). It is a symbol of the powerful west wind thunderstorms that bring rain

---

7. Eagle Man, Ed McGaa *Mother Earth Spirituality* pages 161 - 175
Atwood, Mary Dean *Spirit Healing - Native American Magic & Medicine* pages 40 - 71
Lake-Thom, Bobby *Spirits of the Earth*

and life, the Great Spirit's earth voice (thunder), the time of communication between the earth and sky.

Butterfly: female fertilizing force. It is an archetype of transformation and cross-fertilization. It carries the pollen from one place to another. A symbol of the center, it brings opposites together by taking a little from here and bringing it there. A symbol of simple transformation, proving a little goes a long way.

Hummingbird: a good luck messenger, it takes our prayers to the Great Creator. The hummingbird is an archetype of doctor and healer. It has the power to travel long distances and is considered very spiritual. It teaches us how to soul travel, to develop psychic powers of the mind and how to be graceful.

Animals

Wolf: associated with the East Wind. Symbol of the Teacher. The wolf seeks adventure, explores, and reports the newfound information. The wolf mates for life, is territorial, dedicated to family, loyal, and courageous. It travels long distances, seeks food through group effort, and is curious.

Buffalo: associated with the Southern direction. Buffalo is the symbol of provisions, shelter, gratitude, sustenance, prayer, life abundance, appreciation and thanksgiving.

Bear: associated with the Southern direction. Bear is a symbol of those who seek earth's medicines. Bear's claws dig into Mother Earth; they gather herbs and roots. The Bear may also symbolize a resurrection by waking from deep hibernation.

Horse: associated with the West Wind. Symbol of the first power of the universe (black horse), first four powers: black, red (roan), white, and yellow horses. Horse is a symbol of a means of communication, and recognition of the great vision.

Polar Bear: associated with the cold North Wind. Symbol of patience, resolution, solitary life, and most of all endurance.

Turtle: symbol of Mother Earth. It is a sacred healer and protector.

It grants long life, wisdom, and good health.

Antelope: serves as a messenger to forewarn us of human behavior. Watch the behavior of the antelope to understand what human behavior you are about to encounter.

Badger: symbol of courage, tenacity, and defense. It is a strong protector, containing warrior power and doctor power.

Coyote: symbol of the creator, trickster or teacher. The coyote is full of magic, shameless tricks and special powers. We learn from his lessons of mistakes and accomplishments.

Elk: symbol of the messenger and a strong protector of women.

Mountain Lion: symbol of good luck and skill in the hunt. It is a protector against other powers or people.

Jaguar: (South American) great shaman. Can be associated with woman or man. It is a symbol of the hero, hunter, and slayer. It plays an important part of the creation myth.

Color Symbolism

Color may be used in various ways within a ceremony. A white wedding gown may symbolize purity in one culture and death in another. A red dress may symbolize good luck in one culture, and in another, red symbolizes lust. Wearing black to a funeral in some cultures is a symbol of mourning. Color symbolism is based on a belief system and its inherited understanding.

The following list of color symbolism is referenced from *Ritual Body Art - Drawing the Spirit*, by Charles Arnold, published by Phoenix Publishing Inc.8

White - color of spirit, purity, nourishment (mother's milk), the sacred, the spirit world, provision, and invocation imagery.

Black - color of the night, power, death, fear of that which must be faced, physical strength, restriction, the unknown, secrecy, magic, powers of woman, and the color of the hero who faces the unknown.

Red - the color of will, blood, birth, life and energy, lust (overwhelming drive), desire, and the color of offering and sacrifice.

Red-violet - combination of the spiritual powers of purple and the forcefulness of red. Color of spiritual warriors, spiritual sacrifice, and those who seek to serve and defend their community.

Red-orange - color of absolute abandon, and passions that flow free and take over.

Orange - color used to raise personal energy. Color of courtship, action, physical exertion, and confrontation. A male color.

Yellow-orange - color of the intellectual revolutionary. It combines intellect with strong forcefulness and power. It is used when presenting new and radical ideas.

---

8. Arnold, Charles *Ritual Body Art* pages 58 - 65

Yellow - color of the mind, intellect, memory, attention, curiosity, imagination, air, breath, and breathing.

Yellow-green - color of new growth, new developments, and new beginnings.

Green - color of realized fertility, growth, life, riches, and security. Color of harmonizing and bringing people to their centers.

Turquoise - color of fluidity, forcefulness, wild nature, female color, and calm acceptance. Color of the change of water combined with the stability of earth.

Blue - color of emotion, openness, and acceptance. Associated with water or sky.

Purple - color of spiritual seeking, royalty, and power in the mundane world.

Pink - color of childhood, attraction, and love (platonic to lust depending on the shade of pink).

Gray - color of other worlds: the borderland between the everyday world and the world of the spirit.

Brown - color of unrealized fertility. Color representing openness for new growth.

Silver - used to represent the moon, lunar, and the feminine.

Gold - used to represent the sun, solar, and the masculine.

Scent Symbolism

Scent plays a strong role in our lives. As a child we build a scent library, equating events and scents: Sunday dinner, mother's perfume, our favorite blanket, a rainy day, fresh cookies, father's cologne, grandmother's house, the family car, new shoes, morning coffee, a campfire, etc. Using scents in ceremonies is a subtle yet powerful way to alter consciousness. This practice is known as aromatherapy. Scents can be utilized to set a mood or to create a certain atmosphere. Fragrances can be aroused by the use of raw plants, oils, or incenses.

A word of caution: certain people have strong reactions, even allergies to various scents especially if applied to the skin.

The following list of scent symbols are referenced from *Ritual Body Art - Drawing the Spirit*, by Charles Arnold, published by Phoenix Publishing Inc.9

Allspice - symbol of accomplishment, sending energy. A scent used to fight and gain, to strive and overcome, and for perseverance and strength.

Almond – symbol of childhood. A calming scent. A base for other scents.

Amber - solar scent of male orientation. A power base.

Apple Blossom - beauty scent. Adds compassion and tenderness. It is a symbol of luminescent beauty, an unborn child, children, daughters, dreams, girls, happiness, joy, love, peace, pregnancy, purification, and wholeness.

Balsam - element of air and young male.

Basil – a scent used for purification of space, harmony, and a sense of family.

Bay – a strong purifier. A remover of ego. A scent of change.

---

9. Arnold, Charles *Ritual Body Art* pages 98 - 111

Birch – a scent of understanding and communication.

Camphor – a stimulant and energizer. It combines elements of air and fire.

Carnation – a healing scent which raises the level of awareness. A scent of childbirth, comfort, initiation, marriage, passage, release of the soul and spirit.

Cedar – a scent of purification, dedication, the feminine, family, friends, honor, perseverance, practicality, protection, stability, strength and unity.

Chamomile – a calming scent.

Chili - repellent, a strong energizer - may irritate lungs.

Cinnamon - draws forth true-will, enthusiasm, and fire. Invocation of the God aspect, male, overcoming, self, strength, victory, and strength to summon.

Clove – invigorating scent. It supplies energy for physical, mental, or spiritual work. Clove oil may burn sensitive skin.

Clover – symbol of the maiden, young lord, and growth.

Coffee - stimulant.

Cucumber – symbol of light, water, cool, or refreshing.

Eucalyptus - raises endurance levels and heals breathing disorders.

Frankincense – protective. dream invocation of God and Goddesses, prayer; a deeply spiritual scent.

Gardenia – calming and purifying. Used to overcome panic or hysteria.

Ginger – a solar scent. It counters listlessness, and supplies energy for physical, mental, or spiritual work. Ginger oil may burn the skin.

Heather - attractant, calming, reinforcing when worn by a woman, strengthens will and resolve when worn by a man.

Honey – symbol of the dedication of one's life to a sacred profession.

Honeysuckle - feminine, relieves tension and fears, grounding. It brings a heightened consciousness to the physical level, and is a mild attractant. Symbol of change, growth, home, protection, provision, removal of suffering, stability, wholeness and wisdom.

Juniper - appeases karma. Symbol of good luck.

Lavender – protective and calming. Symbol of air, healing, offering, order, past and wholeness.

Lemon – used for clear dreams, a zest for life, an excitement for living and enthusiasm. Symbol of air, decrease of flow, travel and wishes.

Lilac - emotionally calming. Symbol of gentle love and acceptance.

Lime – a cleanser. It adds vitality.

Lotus – symbol of altered consciousness, deep meditation, increased psychic awareness, increase of flow, intuition, release of the soul, spirit and the flow of water.

Magnolia - overcomes all resistance, a seducer.

Mint - calming agent and purifier. Mint oil may cause burning or irritation.

Mistletoe – a symbol of courting. Indicates interest.

Musk - sensual scent. A symbol of primitive aspects, raising power, attraction, the earth, female, learning, offering, sexual union and fertility.

Myrrh - alters levels of consciousness. A symbol of childbirth, dreams, female, flow, moon and the goddess. It is mildly protective of the psyche and the body.

Narcissus - mystical scent to speed a seeker on their journey. A symbol of change, death, disruption, future, invocation, learning and wisdom.

Nutmeg - solar scent. Strengthens will.

Orange Blossom - sweet purifying scent. A symbol of softness, children, daughter, girls, happiness, joy, love and wholeness.

Orchid - attractant of divine attention and stimulus of spiritual power.

Patchouli – attractant. An earth scent. Symbol of plant fertility, growth, harvest, the present, stability, strength and male.

Peony - power of gentle persuasion.

Pine - cleansing, clears the mind and frees the soul. Symbol of air, boys, enthusiasm, healing, honor, intuition, learning, purification, removal of suffering, volunteer and a soaring spirit.

Rose – attractant. Magical work.

Rosemary – cleanser and purifier.

Sandalwood – a symbol of purity, religious offering, intuition, movement, present, and retreat. It elevates the soul and provides strong protection.

Sweet grass – purifier. A physical form of prayer.

Vanilla - attractant.

Violet – softening. It brings about physical, emotional or spiritual peace.

Wintergreen – analgesic. A symbol of air and winter.

Witch Hazel – purifier and a calming agent.

Ylang-ylang – sensual. Sexual attractant. Attracts passion. A symbol of attraction and desirability.

Journey to Hidden Worlds

A journey to another world is an exploration of changing consciousness. It is the back-woods camper who trades his office environment for a connection with nature, the visitor to foreign lands for a culturally unique view of life, the deep-sea diver who exchanges the solidity of earth for a watery dimension and the shaman who explores a doorway to the spirit world. All of these people are journeying to initiate contact with places of power. Those who initiate this journey in a purposeful way, do so in order to visit the realms of spirit, and to function with the skills and understanding necessary for existence in that world. In terms of ritual, hidden worlds are categorized as either upper (hidden above the earth), middle (on the earth but invisible) or lower (beneath the earth) worlds.

Upper World Entries. Portals for upper world journeys are at the end of a path or route that leads through a hole in the sky. Rays of sunlight, a rainbow, a pathway of smoke, a magical tree or vine are some of the various routes that a spirit can travel upon to enter the upper world.

Lower World Entries. Portals for lower world journeys are those which open into the earth. Caves, tree roots, a spring or well, an opening between stones, an invisible entry behind a waterfall are common routes to a magical lower world existing beneath the earth.

Middle World Entries. Entries into the "between" world require an expansion of consciousness to reveal spirits hidden in the invisible world around us. Spirits of rocks and trees, landscapes, daydreams, fire, water, air, and animals - all of the elements of our daily life are waiting for our discovery.

Basic Steps to Other World Journeys:

1. Relax your body. Take slow deep breaths.
2. Repeat the intention of the journey to yourself three times.
3. Visualize your entry into the Other World.
4. Enter the portal to the Other World (walk down the steps, open a door, climb a ladder).
5. Call your guide to join you (power animal, goddess, or ancestor).
6. Allow your guide to assist you in the purpose of your journey. Receive teachings or gifts.
7. When the purpose of your journey has been achieved, say goodbye to your guide.
8. Return through the portal.
9. Slowly allow the scene to fade as you fully return to your present surroundings.

Chakras

Chakras are energy centers located in the human body. Chakra means "circle" or "wheel," and is often visualized in the form of a lotus mandala. These psychic energy centers are located along the human axis, the spine. The number of Chakras varies according to the specific tradition, numbering anywhere from five (Hopi, Tibetan) to seven (Hindu, Western) energy centers. The flow of energy also varies according to tradition, either drawing down energy from above, or raising energy from the earth. Within each energy center lies a function associated with human action. Instead of haphazard activation of these functions, humans must learn to consciously activate each center, understanding the forces of power that lie dormant within. Any "hooks" into these centers of energy keep us focused outside of ourselves and weakens our connection to these energy centers.

Grounding. Before attempting to work with energy centers, it is a good idea to create a point of "grounding," a centered point of connection with the earth. Excess energy can be sent to, drawn from, or cleansed by the earth. To ground themselves, a person must relax all tension within the body. Taking a series of slow, deep breaths can do this. After feeling a connection to the floor, ground, chair, or wherever the body contacts the earth, a visualized "golden cord" is extended down into the center of the earth. This cord is then "attached" to the earth's center. The energy from the center of the earth is then brought up, through the golden cord, into the body.

First Chakra: Red. Located at the base of the spine (the Mortal Gate). Connection to the earth. Grounding. Security. Point of origin. Anything that represents security (house, bank account,

job, or partner) can be a hook into the first Chakra.
Healing affirmation: "I am safe."

Second Chakra: Orange. Located beneath the navel (the Stove, lower abdomen). Anything that represents the life force. Emotions. Feelings. Sexuality. Creative energy. Definition of the male/female self. Shutting down emotions, unwilling to express feelings, feeling others emotions, sex as primary connection to another, ideas about masculine and feminine identity can be hooks into the second Chakra.
Healing affirmation: "I am centered."

Third Chakra: Yellow. Located at the solar plexus (the Throne of the Creator). Power. Boundaries. Limiting our own behavior. Claiming ourselves. Any person place or thing that represents power (unwilling to establish boundaries, making boundaries stick, offender behavior, money, fame, job, people in authority) can be a hook into the third Chakra.
Healing affirmation: "I am powerful."

Fourth Chakra: Green. Located in the center of the chest (the House of Fire, the heart). Connection to others. Completion within ourselves. Interaction within groups of people. Depending on others, having them depend on us in order to be complete, being at war with ourselves can be hooks into the fourth Chakra.
Healing affirmation: "I am connected."

Fifth Chakra: Blue. Located at the base of the throat. Center of speech, breath and sound. Communication. How we send and receive information from the world. Any time we are unwilling to tell the truth, when we filter reality, when we share inappropriately, the messages we give ourselves can be hooks into the fifth Chakra. Healing affirmation: "I am honest."

Sixth Chakra: Indigo. Located at the forehead, above the eyebrows (third eye, mind, and brain). Center of knowing. Rationalization. Intelligence. Information through intellect. Anything that tells us what to think, judges our thought processes, depending solely on intellect, belief systems around intuitive information are hooks to the sixth Chakra.
Healing affirmation: "I am certain."

Seventh Chakra: Lavender. Located at the top of the head (the Doorway). Connection with spirituality. Relationship with the universe. Anything that tells us who we are, who we are supposed to be, what your purpose in life are hooks to the seventh Chakra.

Healing affirmation: "I am sacred."

The complete energy flow through the Chakras (Hindu) begins with raising energy from the earth through the base of the spine (first Chakra). This fiery energy from the center of the earth is raised up the body along the spine. As it flows through each of the energy centers, the energy carries the color and function associated with each Chakra. The energy flows through the top of the head (seventh Chakra), pouring a rainbow-colored fountain around the body. Spirit energy from the universe (the warmth of the sun) is drawn down through the top of the head, filling the entire body with a warm glow as the energy travels back down to the earth. This two-way energy flow keeps the person connected to the spiritual power of the universe, and cleanses the flow of energy by a grounded connection to the earth's center.

The Wheel of the Year

Seasonal Celebrations - The Sabbats

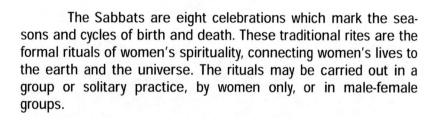

The Sabbats are eight celebrations which mark the seasons and cycles of birth and death. These traditional rites are the formal rituals of women's spirituality, connecting women's lives to the earth and the universe. The rituals may be carried out in a group or solitary practice, by women only, or in male-female groups.

Sabbat	Date	Celebration
Winter Solstice (Yule)	Dec. 20 -23	Longest Night, Ascent
Candlemas	Feb. 2	Purification
Spring Equinox	Mar. 20 - 23	Bursting Forth
Beltane (May Day)	May 1	Sexuality, Fertility, Bloom
Summer Solstice	June 20 -23	Shortest Night, Fulfillment
Lammas	Aug. 1	First Fruits
Autumnal Equinox	Sept. 20 -23	Balance, Harvest
Hallows Eve (Samhain)	Oct. 31	Thin Veil Between Worlds

Winter Solstice (December 20 - 23)

Winter Solstice is the longest night of the year. It is a time to celebrate the darkest night and the deepest winter before the sun's rebirth and awakening of new life. It is the moment in the womb before the birthing process begins and the void before the universe is created. In goddess celebrations, this is the time when Innana begins her return from the underworld.[10] The goddess returns from death to life, Hecate releases Persephone to Demeter, Mary births Jesus, and Tammuz is reborn. From the chaos of nothing comes the birth of all hope and potential. Winter Solstice rituals reflect the passage into the underworld, and the awakening from death to life.

---

[10] Stark, Marcia & Stern, Gynne *The Dark Goddess - Dancing with the Shadow* pages 28 - 41
Wolkstein, Diane & Kramer, Samuel *Innana, Queen of Heaven and Earth*
Stein, Diane *The Women's Spirituality Book* pages 82 - 84

Candlemas (February 1)

Candlemas is a time of purification in preparation for spring. It is a feast of returning light, a time to nurture the flame born at Winter Solstice. It is a time of healing and forgiveness, a time where winter and death are cleansed away, a time to nurture inspiration and creativity, a time of passage into new realms, a dedication to the Road of Life. The way must by paved, the spirit purified, the heart purged to make room for the blessings of spring.11

Spring Equinox (March 20 - 23)

Spring is the time of realizing the potentials of the Winter Solstice and Candlemas. It is a time of bursting forth and childhood. Flowers blossom. Light and dark are balanced. Light is ascending. The cosmic egg is hatching. Jesus returns to his holy self. Persephone returns to earth. Demeter rejoices. The child within is affirmed.

Beltane (May 1)

Weaving of life. The Sacred Marriage. Time of courtship and pursuit. A dance of fertility for the grain. A time of celebrating the first menstruation. Beltane is a time of celebrating sexuality, life-giving fertility, and intimacy between woman and man, each other and the universe. In the Beltane fire dance, each participant jumps over the fire one time, releasing to the flames, something to be banished by love. Then the participant jumps over the flames a second time, this time to draw a love wish from the energy of the fire.

Summer Solstice (June 20 - 23)

Summer Solstice is the shortest night of the year. It is the

[11.] Stein, Diane *The Women's Spirituality Book* pages 84 - 86
Cunningham, Nancy Brady *I am Woman by Rite* pages 6 - 11

time when Innana begins her descent to the underworld, Persephone makes her entrance into Hecate's realm, death and ending are eminent but not yet realized, the earth is at her fulfillment of abundance. Summer Solstice rituals reflect aspects of fulfillment, maturity, and entrances into the unknown.

Lammas (August 1)

Lammas is the celebration of first fruits, green corn, and the ending of summer. It is a time to assure the harvest, which is nearly ripe, but still vulnerable to weather and change. Demeter stops life's blooming in her grief, as Persephone has entered the underworld labyrinth. Lammas is a time to focus on things to come, as winter comes to claim the waning light of summer.

Fall Equinox (September 20 - 23)

Fall, similar to the Spring Equinox, balances equally the light of day and night. Fall Equinox rituals focus on earth celebrations, harvest, plenty, and reproduction from harvest seeds. In the goddess tradition, this is the time when Demeter mourns for her daughter Persephone, and Ishtar mourns for her consort Tammuz. The year is waning. Winter is approaching. The gift of autumn is her abundance.

Hallows Eve (October 31)

Hallows Eve is the time to understand the underground labyrinth of darkness. It is at this time of death that the beginning of life may begin. Persephone travels the labyrinth of the underworld to live with Hecate. From this death, Persephone is conceived again in the womb of Demeter. It is the time when the veil of separation between life and death, between the born and the unborn is at its thinnest. It is the meeting place of beginnings and endings. This time of year is marked for acknowledging the dead, remembering ancestors, and lying to rest the "ghosts," unhealthy patterns or influences. Hallows Eve rituals focus on composting the old into new and more vital forms.

Moon Rituals

Moon Rituals

At the onset of a moonstorm
The temperature changes
The sky turns dark
The wind kicks up dust into
Swirls of potential damage.
Full moon:
Uterus lined, filled,
Stomach changing shape,
Filling, rounding to the point
Between visual and calendar fullness.

Before she shrinks to a sliver,
She will light the night,
Stir emotions
Close to or over the edge.
She has her excuse as we have ours.
All fingers point to the fullness of the cycle
For the madness that ensues.

I hint at stain.
She hints at light.
Together we shall turn the world
Upside down in goddess fashion,
While others will shrug it off
As that time.

Moon Rituals

The word "month" is a reference to the measurement of time between re-occurring cycles of the moon. The phases of the moon affect both ocean tides and human emotions. The female menstrual cycle follows intervals similar to that of the moon. The waxing moon is increasing in light from the new moon to the full moon. The waning moon is decreasing in light from the full moon to the next new moon. Each phase takes approximately a week to transition to the next. The length of the full moon includes the time three days before and after the actual full moon date.

The moon is the embodiment of the goddess in all of her forms. In her time of waxing, she is the Maiden, the daughter, new-born Persephone, Diana and Gaia, and Astarte newly risen from the sea. In her time of fullness, she is the Mother, maturity, peace, power and abundance; she is Demeter, Yemaya, Spider Woman, Ishtar, and Ashtoreth. In her time of waning, she is the Crone, dark aspects, the grandmother, wisdom, aging, endings transitioning into beginnings; she is Hecate, Inanna, Shaman, and Wisewoman.

Moon rituals are central to women's spirituality. Often these rituals are practiced individually, or practiced with a close woman friend. Most calendars contain moon phase date. To obtain more specific information of lunar times and dates, a lunar calendar is required.12

---

12. Stein, Diane *The Women's Spirituality Book* pages 107 - 109

Honoring a Woman's Moon Time

A woman's monthly cycle contains a unique opportunity for introspection. Once a month, our bodies undergo a cleansing. An old uterus lining is sloughed off and a reproductive cycle ends. Along with the bodily changes of hormones and mineral levels, women's emotions are also different at this time. Many tribal cultures understood women to hold a different power at this time of month, and they would not be allowed to mingle with the rest of the tribe. The women experienced a time of rest, of introspection and meditation.

Modern women tend to continue their normal routine at menstruation, ignoring the vast bodily and emotional changes occurring within. PMS (premenstrual syndrome) has become a major issue. "*As hormones change, the level of minerals such as potassium, calcium, and magnesium drop. Women feel these changes in their bodies and their psyches. With the drop in certain minerals and also B vitamins, such as B-6, women naturally feel more tense and anxious, more sensitive and vulnerable. When they know that they have to continue their daily routine for the five or six days before and during their menstrual period, they experience increased anxiety, accounting for the cramps, headaches, low blood sugar, and other symptoms present before the onset of one's moon time.*"13 Elements of a moon time ritual for women need to include supplemental vitamins and minerals, balancing emotional energy, rest, and solitude for contemplation.

Supplements:
> *Like a warrior preparing for battle*
> *My body robs me of precious things.*
> *It gathers blood and tissue, vitamin and mineral*
> *Placing them in a uterine savings account,*
> *For another month of spending.*

Women do not have to become victim to bodily changes.

---

13. Stark, Marcia *Women's Medicine Ways* page 16

PMS symptoms can be alleviated through supplementing the vitamins and minerals lost to monthly hormonal change. Taking extra B vitamins and potassium-magnesium supplements will help. *"...Drinking herb teas that balance hormones (red raspberry leaf, squawvine, and sarsaparilla root). Sarsaparilla root simmered with licorice root or black cohosh can be drunk a few days before menstruation. The Chinese herb dong quai is also excellent to use during the month, a few times a week, preferably simmered as a tea, though it can be obtained in capsules and tablets. Evening primrose oil capsules work well to balance hormones."*14

Balancing emotional energy:

> *At the onset of a moonstorm*
> *The temperature changes*
> *The sky turns dark*
> *The wind kicks up dust into*
> *Swirls of potential damage...*

The physical and the emotional work in concert every month. Taking vitamin and mineral supplements help. Daily exercise also helps. Meditation to focus on grounding can help balance energy. Wearing a moonstone is also said to help balance emotional energy. Tuning in to emotional changes instead of ignoring them becomes a powerful learning tool.

Rest and reflection:

> *In capital letters: R.E.S.T.*
> *A precious commodity in our daily routine.*
> *What would we find if we searched there?*
> *Jewels in the mirror,*
> *I suspect.*

Before we begin a new day we rest from the old one. Menstruation is often associated with the dark phase of the moon, a time of endings and reflection. Emotional vulnerability lends

---

14. Stark, Marcia *Women's Medicine Ways* page 16

opportunity for personal reflection. What do we have the chance to get rid of? Old thoughts, relationships, habits, or longings? What will your new hopes be for the next cycle? What will you do different? Envision all of the poisons (emotional and physical) from the past month being cleansed from your body.

Menarche

In the changing cycles between birth and death, a young woman's first menstrual period is a celebration of the possibility of new life. A menarche ritual prepares the young woman for physical and emotional changes in process or about to occur. Women who participate in the ceremony have the opportunity to heal ugly or painful experiences that they may have gone through themselves.

From *I Sit Listening To The Wind*, by Judith Duerk:

"How might your life have been different if, once long ago, when you were aware of stirring within yourself, of something not yet emerged...there had been a place to go wherever you could sense the presence of an ancient Feminine wisdom? If you sat in the darkness watching as the fires were lighted...and saw the dancing shadows on the walls of the chamber...and were aware, again, of those stirrings within yourself that you could not express?

If the women gathered there around you had affirmed, with shining eyes, that your stirrings were a part of the Feminine most sacred and mysterious...that women of all epochs have instinctively know must remain forever free...How might your life be different?"[15]

Preparation: Before the ceremony, make or purchase a special dress or robe for the young woman. Make a crown or wreath of flowers for her hair. Create a sacred space for the ceremony, including an altar with elements from the four directions.

Materials: Flowers and candles of red and white. Gifts for the young woman. Scented oil or corn meal for self-blessing. A moonstone pendant for the young woman. East is the direction of air, pure thoughts and inspiration. The East can be symbolized with a feather. South is the direction of fire, passion, and the flow of blood. The South can be symbolized with a red candle. The West

---

[15.] Duerk, Judith *I Sit Listening To The Wind* page 61

is the direction of water, the depth of intuition and the waters of the womb. The West can be symbolized with a seashell. The North is the direction of the earth, strength, and the ending of innocence. The North can be symbolized with a white scarf.

Ceremony. Menarche is a ritual of meaning focused toward the young woman. The mother of the young woman presents her daughter to the group of women. The young woman is to be the center of attention throughout the ceremony. The older women are accepting her as a woman among themselves. The young woman learns of women's secrets and responsibilities. She learns about choices, information, and history. She learns to accept and honor the changes in her body, as well as she learns to respect the responsibilities that go along with it. A meditation or creative visualization, poetry, the sharing of women's stories, fears, and celebrations make up the body of the ceremony.

Menopause

When the hormone estrogen reaches a level that is too low to maintain the menstrual cycle then menopause begins. At this time, the ovaries stop producing monthly eggs and estrogen. It is one of the most powerful times in a woman's life as she finds herself moving into the wise woman or crone phase of her life.

Older women become the keepers of wisdom and traditions in the families and communities. "*When a woman leaves the mothering phase and enters Grandmother consciousness, she takes on a new sense of freedom. Mothering, whether it be one's physical children, clients or friends, requires a lot of close attention and dedication of large amounts of energy. Grandmothering, however, is different in that the grandmother's arms are wider (more wisdom), but farther away. She has paid her dues, so to speak, given her time as mother, healer, therapist, counselor. And though she may continue to do so, she does it in a different way – with more detachment, with more freedom for herself.*"16

Sexual freedom is often experienced. The concern to impress others through correct dress codes diminishes. With this new freedom comes the opportunity to express creatively. With the creative freedom comes a sense of wildness and release. Elements of a menopause ritual include planting new seeds, acceptance into the wise woman phase of life and honoring the Crone. Crone goddesses are called into the ceremony: Hecate, Kali, Spider Grandmother, Oya, Ceridwyn, Baba Yaga, and Hella are but a few. Women who are already seasoned in the menopause phase welcome their new sisters into the circle of Wise Women.

---

16. Starck, Marcia *Women's Medicine Ways* page 68

New Moon

From the quiet darkness of night
A small sliver of light.
Not enough to see,
But there is hope...

The new moon is women's invitation to the darkness. As she looks into the depths of her inner most self, a sliver of joy and excitement begins to shine. The old has ended and the changes offer new opportunities. All things become available in the potential. The ending menstrual cycle of the waning moon has left the woman without child and in her Maiden state. New moon rituals are a time of dedication, a time to affirm choice and free agency. It is a time for a woman to take responsibility for her body and actions, to enter into the unknown, a time of self-knowledge and self-love.17

The Full Moon

In the darkness of night,
A glorious display of grandeur.
The heavens above are filled.
The earth below celebrates...

A woman in her full moon phase is at the height of her choices, strength and power. She is the Mother who has accepted or rejected the beginnings of new life. She is the creator of her own paths. She is a goddess of sexuality. She is fertility (self-decisions, conception of creativity), birth (source of life for herself and others), and abundance. Full moon rituals are a time to draw down the power of the fullness of the moon: to take a thought form from the universe and to create a material form here on earth.18

---

17. Stein, Diane *The Women's Spirituality Book* page 110
18. Stein, Diane *The Women's Spirituality Book* pages 113 - 118

The Waning Moon

Once again,
Celebration and laughter
Quietly fade.
The darkness,
Folds her arms around the night...

Women must learn to embrace the ebb as well as the flow. Women must learn to trust that something new is about to begin when they let go of the old. The waning moon is Grandmother, Sage, Crone, Shaman, and Wisewoman. She carries the wisdom gained by experience and transformation. She has died and has been reborn many times. This time of darkening is a time of gathering, of finishing what was begun at the time of the waxing moon. Waning moon rituals are those of healing, protecting, banishing, purification, breaking unhealthy patterns, and releasing what no longer serves.[19]

[19.] Stein, Diane *The Women's Spirituality Book* pages 118 - 122

Rites of Passage

From Cradle to Grave – Rites of Passage

The four major stages of life: birth, coming of age, marriage and death are known traditionally as rites of passage. Such changes in status affect the entire community in which a person lives. Transitions in human life are stressful. This stress translates into the community. Ceremonies to honor life changes alleviate the anxieties surrounding the transition, and keep community stress to a minimum.

Historically, rites of passage have been religious rites, presided over by a priest or priestess, taking place on "sacred" ground. Religious aspects of these rituals give a special power to the transitions. The Divine is called into the ceremony in recognition of particular beliefs. The entire community participates in the ritual, clear instructions are given, and social expectations are adhered to. In this way social disruption is prevented.

The common structure found in most rites of passage rituals can be divided into three phases: separation, transition and re-incorporation. In the first phase, the initiate is cut off from his or her old role in the social structure. During the next phase, the initiate undergoes a period of adjustment and transition from one status to the next, often involving some sort of physical transformation. In the last phase, the initiate is able to rejoin the social structure with his or her new social status.

Rites of Passage - Birth

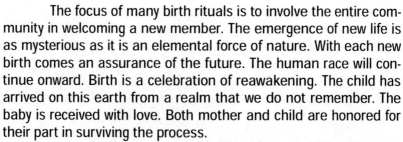

The focus of many birth rituals is to involve the entire community in welcoming a new member. The emergence of new life is as mysterious as it is an elemental force of nature. With each new birth comes an assurance of the future. The human race will continue onward. Birth is a celebration of reawakening. The child has arrived on this earth from a realm that we do not remember. The baby is received with love. Both mother and child are honored for their part in surviving the process.

In our modern thinking, the birth process has changed to a high-tech method of treating an illness, instead of a natural and powerful process to celebrate. As with any great miracle, there is much room for something to go wrong. The technological process of childbirth communicates a necessity to control the natural process of childbirth due to our lack of trust in nature. To further explore this whole concept, I would suggest reading the book *Birth as an American Rite of Passage*, by Robbie Davis-Floyd. She has detailed every step in the birth process, the physiological effects, women's responses and the ritual purposes behind each step.

Pregnancy

In the warm darkness
A seed of light begins to glow.
Created from choice and mutual consent
A new world begins.
Once begun, cannot be undone
A new song to the universe.

"At pregnancy, the woman has chosen to create new life, to accept the role of the Mother Goddess. Her choice is not only for the nine months of gestation and the labor and risks of childbirth, but for the twenty years and more of child-rearing, protecting, teaching, and nurturing that follows."[20]

---

[20] Stein, Diane *Casting the Circle, A Women's Book of Ritual* page 168

"A women's pregnancy ritual is the Women's Spirituality equivalent of the modern baby shower, but with far more depth and meaning. The ritual recognizes the mother-to-be's choice to make a life-changing rite of passage, her entrance into motherhood as the Mother Goddess. The women offer her blessings for 'a safe birth, a strong child, and happiness in motherhood."[21]

During the later stages of pregnancy, many cultures encourage women to reduce her normal activities and to take more rest. As a means of the first phase of a rite of passage (separation), the pregnant mother will often eat different food than the rest of society. Food restrictions are sometimes recommended, not only for nutritional reasons, but that the outward shape or characteristics of certain foods will have effects on the eater. Twinned fruit or rabbit meat may be associated with multiple births, or chewing gum, which is thought to make the placenta stick to the mother's womb.

Pregnancy rituals involve aspects of fertility and protection. They honor beginnings based on choice, and the courage to continue until completion. Pregnancy rituals mark the transition to a new sense of responsibility, from that of the free-spirited Maiden to the Mother who will experience great changes in her life as a result of her decision. Aspects of this ritual may also be used to signify the beginning of any creation - a new job, following a dream, or starting a business.

Birthing

I planted a seed in the darkness
Knowing not what shape it would take,
Or if it would survive the long winter months,
Or if it would have the strength to break through
The darkness into light.

Today, you have heeded the path of centuries.
I hold you in my arms, finally.
After months of silent communication
You take our air into your lungs,

---

[21] Stein, Diane *Casting the Circle, A Women's Book of Ritual* page 173

And let us know
That you are alive

The birth process has traditionally taken place in relative seclusion, and usually only in the presence of other women. Only in recent times has the western culture accepted that the male partner has a role during delivery.

Due to the role of hospitals in the birthing process, there may not be a lot of room left to create your own "rituals" while participating in the medical routine. The ultimate natural experience would be to deliver the baby at home, with a midwife and to be surrounded by people that you trust and love. Nature being what it is, the best-planned experience may never occur. The point is to connect with the divine in some way, even if it is a quick prayer while you are delivering the child in the back seat of a taxicab.

Cleansing

Separated by skin
We have known each other,
Like pen pals that are to meet
For the first time.
They wash from your skin
The road-dust of your travel.
Warmth upon warmth,
Our eyes with one common gaze.

Ritual cleansing of the newborn child was the tradition of the woman who received the baby during labor. The baby is cleansed with water or milk, wrapped in animal skin or cloth, and placed next to the mother. Western traditions vary by region. Numerous hospitals cut the umbilical cord, clean and take the babies measurements before letting mother and child bond for the first time.

Blessing or Naming Ceremonies

We take this child in our arms,
To give it a name and a blessing.
By this name, the child shall be known.

"*The newborn baby is not instantly and automatically a member of society. His or her entry into society is usually marked by some special ceremony. In some cases this might be little more than a formal announcement that the birth has taken place...The formal acceptance of the new infant as a member of society frequently involves a ritual in which the child is given a name. The ceremony can identify the child and make public his or her parentage. It may also signal the child's entry into the local religion, and magic may be performed to protect the child from evil spirits. The ritual may lay down the responsibilities of the parents and others in looking after the child. In some cases, the naming ceremony also serves to mark the return of the mother to normal society after her confinement.*"22

In religious ceremonies, the blessing or baptism ritual re-enacts the birth process in some way. Oftentimes, water is an essential part of the ceremony. In Christian religions, using water in the ceremony is to symbolize the baptism of Christ, or to symbolize rebirth. Water is only one of the elements used to welcome the newborn child into the community. Other cultures may invoke the element of "fire" by using smoke to purify the infant or the sun by holding the baby high in the sunlight.

Blessing or naming rituals invoke wishes of protection and good fortune for the new baby as it begins its journey on this earthly plane.

---

22. Ingpen, Robert & Wilkinson Phillip *A Celebration of Customs &Rituals of the World* pages 54 - 56.

Re-entering Society

After the miracle
Then what?

In many societies there is a relative isolation period for the mother after giving birth. Much of this time is spent bonding with her new baby. When this time has been completed the mother is accepted, once again, into the community.

In some religions, this happens through the church where she gives prayers of thanks to God for surviving the "pain and peril of childbirth." In other societies, the women in considered to be impure or polluted from the childbirth experience. A period of cleansing must occur before the woman can be integrated into society. In Western culture, the mother spends a defined amount of time in the hospital, a number of weeks at home, and a release from her doctor before she is to return to society.

The time after a baby is born is a "forgotten" time for countless new mothers. Many experience postpartum depressions due to the fact that the excitement is over and reality has now set in. She may now feel the exclusion of past activities due to fatigue, recovery, or lack of relief.

Rituals for re-entry into society are crucial to this new mother so that her experience will not be perceived as such an affliction. This is the time for the Crone (an experienced mother or grandmother) to assist the transitioned mother into her new role.

Coming of Age - Spiritual Adulthood

The transition from child to adult admits the initiate into a new social sphere from which he or she was previously excluded. If there is no transitioning ceremony to mark the passing from childhood into adulthood, it is like driving to a foreign country without knowing you crossed the border and without understanding the rules of the region. An individual passing from childhood into adulthood experiences bodily changes, new social privileges and responsibilities. The world of childhood is suddenly divided between male and female, and expectations shift towards that of the adult realm.

Within tribal societies the initiate often experiences a form of bodily hardship (mutilation or marking of the body) and/or educational experience to prepare the individual for adult life. Male individuals may undergo a test of strength, endurance or courage. Girls have coming of age rituals centered around their first menstruation, after which she is considered to be a full member of the tribe or society, possibly ready for marriage and women's responsibilities. The timing of such ceremonies varies, depending upon age, social status or puberty. The general pattern for coming of age ceremonies is the 3 stages of separation, transition, and reincorporation.

Separation: The individual is separated from the state that he or she is leaving behind. The initiates may be taken into the wilderness, taken to a place apart from the main village, or removed from the designated children's play area.

Transition: The individual is introduced to the new group that he or she will be joining. The initiate may undergo a "drama" where he or she is dying to the old way and being reborn into a new status. Permanent body marking may be performed to clearly differentiate those who have not been through the coming of age ceremony. Body paint, colored clothing, or masks may be used as symbols of entering into adulthood. Some ordeal or education must occur before the initiate can move on to the next social state.

Re-incorporation: A ceremony occurs to publicly confirm the fact that this member has joined the adult society. Feasting, dancing, or performing an action demonstrates to the rest of the society that the initiate is ready to carry out his or her new responsibilities.

Coming of age, in Western culture, has often been marked by high school graduation or receiving the "keys to the car." Sweet sixteen or debutante balls have marked the dating potential of teenage girls. Bar Mitzvah and Bat Mitzvah celebrations mark the Jewish boy or girl's coming of age. A new movement toward wilderness "survival skill" training or "Vision Quests" is being advertised as coming of age rituals for teens. Proms, body piercing, formal balls, initiation into gangs, and entry into the military are often seen as modern forms of coming of age ceremonies.

Rites of Passage - Marriage

Marriage is one of the most festive rites of passage. It signals one of the key turning points in the vast majority of adult lives. The joining of two lives in marriage affects not only themselves, but the surrounding community as well. There will be repercussions for both sides of the family, binding alliances, property and traditions, or creating completely new ones. The ceremony itself is a reflection of social values, with the couple affirming the social order by participation in tradition. The main focus of the marriage ceremony is often a mixture of legal and religious aspects, providing a "contract" which sets out the rites and duties of the couple, and "proof" that the union is recognized by both church and state. Key aspects of the marriage ceremony include preparation, ceremonial dress, procession, bonding, feasting, dancing, and gift giving.

Preparation: Before the actual ceremony begins there are many tasks of preparation. There are formal dinners where the two families meet for the first time, parties to signify the ending of "single" status in the community, making or selecting the wedding attire, and a time of instruction to prepare for upcoming changes.

Ceremonial Dress: The ceremonial dress of the bride and the groom distinguish them from the rest of the crowd. The couple is to be the center of attention for an event that is about to affect the rest of the community. Customs and traditions place meaning on color and style to promote feelings of good luck, prosperity, fertility, and purity.

Processions: The purpose of processions varies from culture to culture. A public procession may be the way to get the whole wedding party from one place to another. It may prepare the community for the upcoming union. It may signal the arrival of the bride or groom, or it may signify the path that each has chosen in order to come together in marriage. In Western culture, when the ceremony is complete the couple ride off in a car decorated with ribbons, balloons, and cans tied to the bumper. Everyone sounds their horns to let the rest of the community know that a couple has been married.

Bonding: At this time, the formal union of the couple is performed. Vows, duties, agreements, rites, religious and social values are woven into the bonding of the couple. These rites are performed before witnesses and sealed with a token of promise by exchanging rings. The union is sanctioned religiously, legally and socially.

Feasting: The extension of this union into the larger community is often celebrated through feasting. Food is a symbol of hospitality; it symbolizes abundance and the basic necessities of life. The entire community shares in the good fortune of the union. Speeches, good wishes and toasts to the couple are shared at the feast.

Dancing: This common feature of the wedding ceremony is an expression of celebration. Dance is a symbol of harmony and the coming together of partners. Often the newly married couple will begin the dance, joined later by the unified family and guests. In this way, the bride and groom have now re-entered society with their new status as a couple.

Gift Giving: Former ceremonies involved a financial agreement between families. A price was paid to the family of the bride or groom to compensate the family for the loss of a laboring individual, or to bring an inheritance to the new family. Modern couples receive well-wishing or congratulatory gifts. Gift giving today involves providing a beginning foundation for the newly married couple to build upon.

Rites of Passage – Death

As inevitable as birth, the difficult and often traumatic human passage, death, is a transition affecting the whole community. There are many challenges for the living that are left behind. Questions about the afterlife, the whereabouts of their loved ones, the task of living life without the departed member and the meaning of life tend to be pondered at this time. Funeral rituals prepare us for the shock of death and help to ease the process of grieving. Without religious belief, death is perceived as an ending. Religious people see death as the beginning of a new phase of existence. Nearly all believe in some sort of "spirit world" waiting for those who pass on to the other side.

Key aspects of funeral rituals include commemorative rites, dressing the body, dress for mourning, the vigil or viewing of the body, burial, and marking the gravesite.

Commemorative rites: Specific customs are attributed to commemorate the passing of an individual. Lowering the flag to half-mast, stopping all clocks to mark the time of death, wearing black armbands, emptying all the water vessels in the house, covering mirrors, and opening windows are all customs of commemoration.

Dressing the body: Many cultures emphasize the correct procedure to prepare the body for burial. Mummification, washing and grooming the corpse, decorating the body with dyes and perfumes, dressing the body in particular clothing or jewelry, and the closing of the eyes are traditional ways of preparing the body for burial.

Mourning dress: By changing their outward appearance, those who are grieving can be distinguished from the rest of society. Clothing of a subdued or black color is traditional for those in the West, in other cultures; white is the traditional color for mourning. Tribal peoples may use special body paint as a symbol of mourning, to disguise themselves from the dead who may return to take friends or relatives away with them.

The vigil: Viewing the body makes public the fact that the person is actually dead. It can be a time to pay one's last respects to the deceased in the comforting presence of family. Being in the close physical presence of death helps those left behind to come to terms with their own eventual passing.

Burial of the dead: Burying the corpse in the earth has been the most common method to entomb the body. Often times prized possessions, a planned route through the underworld, tools, cooking utensils; coins or weapons were buried with the body for use in the next world. The site for burial is often considered to be holy or consecrated ground.

Marking the gravesite: Marking the site of burial is a way to keep the memory of the deceased alive. The marker becomes a point of focus for those who wish to honor or remember the dead. Flowers, candles, written prayers or memorials, and religious symbols are used to mark the gravesite.

Dancing As Ritual

Dancing As Ritual

When we think of modern dancing, we tend to think of smoky bars, loud music, women in groups on one side, men on the other, manipulation, seduction, a place where "dancing" is secondary to finding a partner to pair up with - at least for one night. In other words, we dance for mere enjoyment and think of it as a pastime.

For ancient peoples, dancing was a ceremonial ritual, a prayer filled with symbolic representation in costume, movement and rhythm. The dancer's feet moved to caress the earth, their body movement and costumes told stories. Dancing was a religious drama and a prayer of gratitude and thanksgiving. Dancing was a request for favors or protection, for success in the hunt, or preparation for battle. The dance was performed with the greatest reverence, with meticulous attention to every detail of the preparation of costume, making of masks, and purifying of the dancers. There were dances to personify the gods, to send messages to the gods, to mark changes in the year and to initiate children into puberty. There were animal dances at the time of the hunt to appease game into sacrificing themselves for the good of their human brothers, medicine dances to cure diseases, the passing on of historical stories, and war dances to increase the strength to win.[23]

---

[23] Fergusson, Erna *Dancing Gods: Indian Ceremonials of New Mexico and Arizona.*

Elements of the Dance

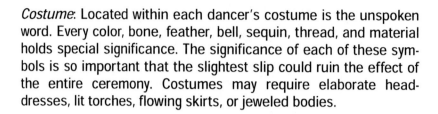

Costume: Located within each dancer's costume is the unspoken word. Every color, bone, feather, bell, sequin, thread, and material holds special significance. The significance of each of these symbols is so important that the slightest slip could ruin the effect of the entire ceremony. Costumes may require elaborate head-dresses, lit torches, flowing skirts, or jeweled bodies.

Rhythm: For those cultures that do not possess harmony in their music, tempo and rhythm become the "song" by combining different rhythms and pauses. The drums may be one rhythm, bells on the dancer's feet another, shells and rattles another, chanting or singing another. When all of these elements combine, the entire song is created. Gabrielle Roth, in her book *Maps to Ecstasy*, teaches us five rhythms which are experimental when a human being explores dance:

> 1. The flowing rhythm: teacher of fluidity and grace.
> 2. The rhythm of chaos: announcement of creativity seeking a form.
> 3. The staccato rhythm: teacher of definition and refinement.
> 4. The lyrical rhythm: teacher of synthesis and integration.
> 5. The rhythm of stillness: teacher of contentment and peace.24

The Body: Many ceremonial dancers are purified before the actual ceremony. As well as practicing for long periods of time, the dancers may fast, bathe, or decorate their bodies with symbols related to the particular ceremony. Ancient Egyptian inscriptions described the arms to be as important as the legs in dance. Greek pottery indicates that motions made by the head and body were necessary in the movement of dance. In the origin of sacred dance, the body was meant to imitate the characteristic of supernatural powers; the swaying of trees, the flowing of rivers, or the movement of animals.25

---

24. Arrien, Angeles *The Four-Fold Way* pages 26 -27

The Dance: Every step and movement has meaning in the prayer or story of ceremonial dance. The footwork is precise; the control of body and breath is masterful. The dance steps may vary widely, including complicated changes of tempo and rhythm, or graceful turns of long rows of dancers. Hours and days of practice for each performance can be intense. Martha Graham said this about practice: " *I believe that we learn by practice. Whether it means to learn to dance by practicing dancing or to learn to live by practicing living, the principles are the same. In each it is the performance of a dedicated precise set of acts, physical or intellectual, from which comes shape of achievement, a sense of one's being, a satisfaction of spirit. One becomes in some area an athlete of God. Practice means to perform, over and over again in the face of all obstacles, some act of vision, of faith, of desire. Practice is a means of inviting the perfection desired.*"

Accompaniment: Drum-beating as an accompaniment to dancing goes hand in hand. It is hard to imagine one without the other. In ritual dance, the drum is never beaten uselessly. Foot stamping, hand clapping, striking a rod, noise makers such as bone or shell rattles, gongs, bells, cymbals, flutes, castanets, chanting, melody, singing are some of the instruments of accompaniment to ritual dance. The accompanying instruments not only assist in rhythm, but they add magic. The manner in which the instrument is played, or the materials used to construct the instrument invite invisible authorities to participate in the ceremony. 26

25. Oesterley, W.O.E. *The Sacred Dance*
26. Sachs, Curt *World History of the Dance* pages 175 - 203

Ritual Dances

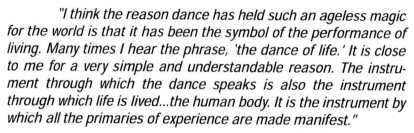

"I think the reason dance has held such an ageless magic for the world is that it has been the symbol of the performance of living. Many times I hear the phrase, 'the dance of life.' It is close to me for a very simple and understandable reason. The instrument through which the dance speaks is also the instrument through which life is lived...the human body. It is the instrument by which all the primaries of experience are made manifest."

- Martha Graham

The Wedding Dance. Wedding dances are found in a great many societies. Ancient wedding or marriage dances usually including some kind of sword dance, in which the bride and groom are protected from external danger. These dances include the bride and groom dancing in the center of an enclosed circle of assembled guests. In modern times, wedding dances are usually kept separate from the wedding ceremony, to keep this more secular ritual apart from the religious. When the ceremony ends, the dancing begins. The just- married couple dance (waltz, slow dance, or jumping over a broom) in front of the assembled guests. To honor the fact that two families have been united, the bride and groom separate and invite the parents to dance. More family members are invited to join in the dance, and then all are invited to join the newly married couple on the dance floor.

Carnival. Carnival has undergone many changes over the years, blending African elements of the coronation of kings and queens, and European elements honoring the Virgin Mary. Today's Carnival is a procession of competing "samba schools." Each samba school creates a pageant based on a patriotic Brazilian theme, stressing ethnic pride and improved relations between the various racial and religious groups, hoping to be judged to be the winners of Carnival for the year.

Initiation Dances. The sacred aspects of these dances vary from culture to culture: to chase away potential demons that threaten the transitioning child at puberty, to generate sexual power, which will assure the tribe of healthy descendants, or to dispel the god-myth of the parents behind the mask. The general flow of initiation ritual dances is the transition of the boy or girl into man or woman-hood. Often times the adults dance in a circle around the boy or girl, a transitioning event occurs, the child symbolically dies, and the adult is awakened. The transitioning event can be a change in dance position from the west to the east, a removal of frightening masks, or a solo dance of exhaustion, which requires the help of adults to complete. Pale versions of these initiation dances occur among modern teens. Teens "transition" into adulthood through simulating adult actions. The junior and senior "proms" serve as a simulation of the adult world; the formal attire, finding a partner, choosing a theme, election of the prom "queen, or renting a limou-sine. The senior prom is a step into the adult world, a statement that these teens are no longer children, that they are making their own decisions that reflect their personal views.

Fertility Dances (vegetation). The chief concern in a fertility dance is to charm the elements into releasing the best circumstances for growing crops. Rain dances fall into this category, as well as dances that revolve around carrying the power of growth to living crops. In the center of the ring of dancers, held in the dancer's hands or adorned on their bodies are the symbols of living branches, vines or grains. The dancer evokes the power of growth to the crop by honoring it with dance. The modern version of the fertility dance is the dance around the Maypole, in which a pole is placed in the ground as a fertility center to be danced around. This central post is decorated with multicolored ribbons or streamers tied to the top of the pole while the dancers hold onto the other end. The dance consists of gaily weaving in and around one other as the dancer's circle around the pole.

Fertility Dances (human). Many vegetation fertility dances begin with the subject of human fertility. Human fertility dances insure the propagation of the tribe, while vegetation fertility dances insure the abundance of food. Ancient peoples did not place a dis-tinction between human activities and the activities of nature. These dances were meant to be erotic and sexual in nature; often artistically including elements of sexual intercourse within the dance. In many cultures, one gender is encircled by another and a selection occurs. Other cultures dance together as couples and then depart two by two into the night. 27

Masked Dances. In masked ritual dances, the dancers conceal their identity. Not only is the dancer's identity concealed, but they give up their own identity by taking on that of the spirit or animal portrayed by the mask. The mask is designed to bear the identifying characteristics of the particular entity, which may be grotesque, frightening, or fantastic. These dances are dramatic; they follow the irrational laws of dream worlds, subconscious minds or the world of fantasy. Lessons of conquering fears were taught to young initiates by the use of mask. Masked dances have been used by medicine men to heal the sick. Cultural history is taught by the dramatic use of masks and costume in ritual dance.

Modern day masquerades have their roots in ritual masked dances. Masquerade balls delight the dancers by allowing them the opportunity to make believe and to trick others by concealing their identity. The dancer is freed from the boundaries of self by concealing his or her face; the body is then free to act the way that the dancer wishes.28

27. Sachs, Curt *World History of the Dance* pages 64 68
28. Sachs, Curt *World History of the Dance* pages 131 - 138

Spirit Dance Ritual

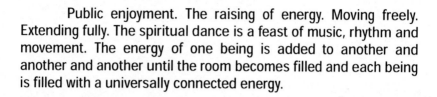

Public enjoyment. The raising of energy. Moving freely. Extending fully. The spiritual dance is a feast of music, rhythm and movement. The energy of one being is added to another and another and another until the room becomes filled and each being is filled with a universally connected energy.

Preparation:
1. Find a large enough space to accommodate the dancers. This could be a rented cafeteria or gymnasium, or a large outdoor clearing.
2. Bless the dancing space.
3. Gather a wide range of music for the event. Select "world" music, ethereal music, fast rhythms, and music with or without vocal accompaniment.
4. Have everyone dress comfortably, in clothes that allow movement.

Materials:
Musical selection
Water

Invocation:
Have everyone join hands, close their eyes, and spend a moment in silence (at least 30 seconds) to draw energy from the center of their bodies. With hands joined and eyes closed, the officiator will offer a spiritual prayer for the raising and uniting of spiritual energies.

Dancing:
Begin with quiet ethereal music. Let the dance be a slow, stretching of the body. This is the time to let go of the outside world, to let go of embarrassment, fear and uncertainty. It may take several songs before the dancers are willing to let go of their protective, isolated energies and begin to unite with the group.
Build the tempo of the music. The body movement will shift from flow to form. Energy will begin to fill the entire room.

Continue to build the tempo of the music. Dancers may break off into smaller groups of four or five members, each with their own energy center, which will then become part of the pattern of the collective whole.

Vary the energy output of the dancers by alternating slow and fast music. Vary from popular music to world music. Feel the energy change like a kaleidoscope view. Sense the energy move past the confines of the dance space to connect with the universe.

Closing:

Slow the music back down to a quiet ethereal tempo. Become aware of the universal connection. Have everyone join hands, close their eyes, and spend a moment in silence. With hands joined and eyes closed, the officiator will offer a closing prayer for the continued connection of spiritual energies.

Drumming As Ritual

Drumming As Ritual

"I come into the drumming circle with my rhythm, with my talk. Somebody else creates a rhythm, and that person will then carry the rhythm. He has the burden to keep the rhythm going. What I do on the drum is my response to what I hear. So I talk back. I drum my feelings. That's my opinion. When somebody else comes in with another drum beat, that is his own opinion. So, we end up with a whole brouhaha of opinions that an outsider might find extremely synchronic and rhythmical or chaotic and noisy. To drum is to hear."[29]   - Malidoma Patrice Some

The drum is alive with Spirit. Created from living materials, the body of a drum carries the spirit of the tree whose trunk the wood was carved from. It also carries the spirit of the animal skin, and the spirit of the person playing the drum. The living tree contains a heartbeat. The living animal contains a heartbeat. The person playing the drum contains a heartbeat. All three spirits combine to form one unique sound. If another drummer sits down to play the same drum the sound will not be the same. The drum is the voice of internal rhythm.

Drumming Energy. Rituals involving drums invoke a large amount of energy. The drumming motion directs energy from the sky to the earth. The energy is then released from the drum and directed in an upward motion back towards the sky. The drummer becomes a conductor of energy flow, a creator of life. Mickey Hart, in his book *Planet Drum*, put it this way: *"The beginning of our universe: mysterious forces came together and space, matter, and time began, with a vibration unlike anything before or since. The big bang, a birth in chaos and din, was beat one."*[30]

Drumming Principles. Every type of drum requires a different set of muscles, motions and energy to release its sound. Hand placement, depth of breath, wrist control, energy focus, stick technique,

---

[29] Some, Malidoma Patrice *Ritual: Power, Healing and Community* page 89

[30] Hart, Mickey & Lieberman, Fredric *Planet Drum* page 11

posture, chant, communication, awareness, cycle orchestration and stroke are only a few of the varied components in drumming. The drummer cannot think his rhythm, it must be felt. The drummer cannot breathe high, fast and shallow, because there will be no room for sensitivity of the spirit. The drummer cannot sit or stand rigid and uptight, because there will be no opportunity for the energy regeneration that comes from fluid movement. The drummer cannot ignore an awareness of the other drums in the circle, otherwise he cannot respond from his inner voice. The drummer must remain aware of tempo, mood changes, intensity and pace. He must flow with these changes like a flock of birds changing direction.

Rhythm. Rhythm is organized noise, it is anything that repeats itself over a period of time: windshield wipers, footsteps, chewing, raindrops, cicadas, frogs, birds, thunderstorms, or hammering. Every molecule and atom has a signature rhythm of movement. Our universe contains an orchestra of synchronized motion; humans connect to this universal heartbeat through the sound of percussion. Notice that when several people walk together, their footsteps seem to fall into a synchronized rhythm. This is what scientists refer to as the law of entrainment. This law states that if two rhythms are nearly the same and their sources are in close proximity, they will always synchronize. The theory behind this law is that it takes less energy to pulsate together than in opposition.[31]

Sacred Drumming. The specifics of most drum rituals are held to be sacred, and are usually confidential. Drumming (or any kind of music) changes people's consciousness. It is not to be taken lightly. Tribal elders or family ancestors have held the specifics of such rituals as gifts to be handed to one who was prepared to handle the sacred aspects of the gift. Modern-day drum circles tend to have a leader (conductor) who understands the voice of each type of drum, and the flow and movement of energy required for the collective drum song. Specific contemporary drum ensembles, such as *Taiko* groups combine spiritual aspects, physical discipline, and precise rhythms to produce an intensely orchestrated marriage of human and percussion.

[31.] Hart, Mickey & Lieberman, Fredric *Planet Drum* page 17

Inner Voice. For those who are "shy," playing the drum can be very intimidating. There is no hiding who you are. There are no false pretenses. The drum will announce what your skin says to its skin, how your energy is released through its energy. Respect the living presence within the drum. Many traditions request the drummer to rub the skin (head) of the drum or to say a prayer to the animal whose life was sacrificed for the drumhead. Initial practice with the drum will be revealing - possibly uncomfortable. "Playing along" with other music will be impossible until you first find your own voice.

How to Begin. Begin with feeling. Start with your heartbeat. Close your eyes; deprive your senses of everything else but the sound, the sound within. Feel your body move, become aware of your breathing, feel the energy flowing through you. Listen to drum music (without playing along with it) of various cultures as you would a symphony. Train your hearing to the rhythms of each percussion instrument. Go to Pow Wow's, Latin, Caribbean, African, or Polynesian festivals, watch a Taiko group perform. Immerse your senses in the world of drumming by participating in local drum circles. Drum circles may be difficult to find at first. The "public" drives many of these drum circles to hidden locations because of "noise ordinances" or public disturbance problems. Check with your local music stores. Someone in the percussion section will be able to get you into contact with a drum circle.

Mandala Ritual

Mandala as Ritual

―――――――――――――――――― ＜◆＞ ――――――――――――――――――

"If man has alienated himself from the source, the center within, then it is the purpose of a Mandala ritual for our time to be used as a primal tool for investigating and opening that center, once again granting the individual an identification with the cosmic forces and their source."   - Jose & Miriam Arguelles

A Mandala is a design symbolizing the universe. The center of a Mandala is the beginning, the first principal. From this central point, a series of symmetric forms (fluid or rigid) and cardinal (compass) points emerge. Examples of Mandalas can be found in various cultures: Navaho sandpaintings, the Aztec Sunstone, the Rose Window and Labyrinth in Chartres Cathedral, Stonehenge, the Hawaiian Solar Flower, the Australian Tjuringa stone and Tibetan Mandala rituals.

"The healing, meditative, integrative purpose of the Mandala has its beginning and its root in man's attempt at self-orientation. Man is the center of his own relative time/space locus from which he receives a cosmic consecration. Whatever is in front, behind, to the left, and right of him become the four cardinal directions; whatever is above and below become the heavens and the earth; what was yesterday and will be tomorrow becomes time past and time future - and the center is always the individual, the bearer of the awareness of the eternal now."[32]

The Navaho use sandpaintings as a physical place for healing. The person being healed sits in the center. Symmetrically placed about the center are symbols of the directions, elements or seasons. A ceremony is performed and then the sandpainting is destroyed. As a method of meditation, constructing a Mandala focuses the meditator in identification with his or her relatedness to universal patterns. This relatedness creates wholeness, the wholeness demonstrates self-healing. Through creation of the Mandala and identification with universal wholeness, the medita-

―――――――――――――――――――――――――――

[32] Arguelles, Jose & Miriam *Mandala* page 15

tor realizes a source of energy within his or herself.

The materials used in Mandala rituals are as individualized as the various cultures themselves. Paint, paper, cloth, colored sand, stone, glass, thread, pencil, chalk, sticks - anything that the imagination can utilize can be applied in the making of a Mandala.

As with all rituals, several defined principles of the Mandala ritual apply:33

1. Purification
2. Centering
3. Orientation
4. Construction
5. Absorption
6. Destruction
7. Reintegration
8. Actualization

Purification. A cleansing of the body is required to remove any blocking of spiritual reception. Often the materials themselves will also be purified to clearly channel spiritual forces.

Centering. Involves a concentration of energies inward, focusing them through a central point. Meditation, handicrafts, breathing exercises - anything that centers the mind to the still point (without form) within.

Orientation. After a centering point has been defined, the consciousness then defines the cardinal points: North, South, East, and West. Defining the cardinal points creates a sacred space; prayers, offerings, dances, or chants then consecrate it. The "Ground of the Mandala" or Holy Circle is consecrated.

Construction. Actual construction of the Mandala can take many forms, clearly defined or loosely implied. The Mandala might be defined by the Cosmic Fortress - a cosmic plan or home of a deity. Symbols of protective bands or entities, a center of power or creation, and the functioning of nature, or by the Transmutation of Demonic Powers - a projection of negative aspects into the

---

33. Arguelles, Jose & Miriam *Mandala* pages 84 - 99

ordered whole in which negative forces are not eliminated but transformed.

Absorption. Absorption requires a contemplation of the completed Mandala. The parts, functions and contents of the Mandala are absorbed into the mind and body of the beholder. The spiritual forces of the Mandala are transferred; the energy projected out is now drawn back in.

Destruction. After absorption comes a phase of detachment from the Mandala. The Navaho destroy their sandpaintings at this phase of the ritual. Most cloth, paper, or woven Mandalas are not physically destroyed but hung in a sacred environment as a meditation. The point is to detach, to remove the attachment of pride from the creation, to remind the participant that they were but a vessel for the Spirit to flow through.

Reintegration. Healing or connection to the spiritual through the ritual of the Mandala has left the participant whole again. They have detached from the Mandala form and are now complete. The participant is now free to directly connect, once again, to his spiritual source.

Actualization. The previous steps of the Mandala ritual are but a prelude to integrate the Mandala form into everyday life. The world is no longer fragmented and divided, but is a dimension of a greater whole. New knowledge has been obtained through the Mandala initiation; the individual is now restored to the vision of wholeness.

Another source of information on the healing art of creating mandalas is *Mandala, Luminous Symbols for Healing* by Judith Cornell. Her book contains many colorful examples and step by step instructions for creating healing Mandalas. For each pattern of mandala, Judith Cornell provides a list of needed supplies, a centering meditation, and instructions for creating each pattern.

The book *Creating Mandalas*, by Susanne F. Fincher contains a great deal of background information about color, animal, shape, and numerical symbols within the mandala pattern. Chapter 6: *The Great Round of Mandala Forms* details the cycles or stages of mandala design.

Body Decoration
as Ritual

Body Decoration as Ritual

————————————<◆>————————————

Body decoration is accomplished through many different forms. Permanent and temporary tattooing, makeup, body piercing, body painting, and even body scarring. Ceremonies for celebrating heroic deeds, priming for war, transitions into adulthood, success in the hunt, acceptance into society, tribal status and preparation for marriage have included some form of body decoration.

Body decoration has been used for disguise, as in modern warfare, where the face is camouflaged so that the soldier blends in with the background. Another use of disguise is to hide one's identity, to be associated with another group, or to hide from the gods or spirits of the enemy. Shamanic body decoration is used to transform the body into the spirit of an animal or deity. Symbolic colors and designs are painted on the body to call upon the spiritual power of the animal or deity.

Modern "primitives" use body decoration for similar purposes as our ancient ancestors. Halloween and costume party disguises, affiliation with groups or gangs, makeup to enhance beauty, decoration, celebrating rites of passage, or camouflage in warfare.

Methods of Body Decoration

Temporary Tattoo: Used as beauty enhancement, the temporary tattoo is a no-risk method of toying with the idea. Children often get temporary tattoos from gum machines, in boxes of cereal or candied popcorn, using them to role-play adult behavior or to adorn their body. Adults may purchase temporary tattoos for adornment, to wear to parties, to enhance an acting role, or as a marking for a ceremony. The tattoo pattern is silk-screened onto a specially coated paper. The coating dissolves when wet, and the design is transferred from the paper to the skin. These tattoos can be removed with baby oil or rubbing alcohol.

Henna Tattoo: Used since early Egyptian times, henna tattoos are transitory methods of beauty enhancement. Henna tattoos are applied mainly to the feet and hands, where the tattoos last longer. The application of henna is a ritual, which can take up to six hours. The hands and feet must be washed with Rose and Orange water before henna application. The henna must be mixed ahead of time: henna powder, a cup of brewed black tea allowed to sit overnight, one teaspoon of fresh lemon juice from a lemon which sat in the sun for twelve hours or more, mixed together in a glass bowl. The paste is applied with a cake decorator bag or a traditional Mishwak pick. After the paste dries, it is brushed off and the resulting designs remain in place for up to four weeks.

Kohl: A black powder used by women of the Arabian Peninsula as eyeliner and eyeshadow. It was believed to have value as a protection against eye disease, and also controlled the sun's glare in the desert. Modern "kohl" eyeliner pencils **cannot** be applied in the same manner as kohl, next to the eye. Kohl is a fine antimony powder applied between the eyelids, actually touching the eye. The eyelids look black around the roots of the eyelashes with no white skin showing.

Tattoo: Over the centuries tattooing has taken on various symbolic meanings. Tattoos have been used as a protection against evil, as a rite of passage into adulthood, initiation into groups or gangs, as protection in battle, and ornamental art. Early man thought of tattooing as a means to bring a person closer to a deity or magical powers, to symbolize the fertility of the earth and of womankind, preservation of life after death, and identity with a clan.

Body Painting: In goddess-centered societies, body painting was an act of worship. Identification and communication with the Goddess through body painting utilized the body as a living prayer to the deity. Used in conjunction with masks, body painting is used in symbolic role-playing ceremonies. Sacred designs and meaningful color systems are combined on the palette of the body to create a living ceremony of worship. Children often mark their bodies with ink or paint as a matter of artistic expression. In the book *Body, The Ultimate Symbol*, Olivia Vlahos writes this about painting the body:

"*Paint binds and separates, defining the pairs of opposites: sacred-profane, male-female, sick-well, good-bad, high-low, living-dead. Paint sets human beings apart from nature, while at* the same time putting them in touch with natural forces appre-hended but dimly understood. *Paint announces the crisis times of life and announces them on the bodies of individuals in stress. By the power and meaning of color, feelings are channeled and vul-nerability protected. By color are companions notified to give sup-port and consolation. In paint a community displays collective values and sustain social commitment. By looking much like everyone else, the individual demonstrates participation and belief in a common identity. Finally, paint communicates on the outer skin something of the inner self. It is a self-enlargement, ide-alized, enhanced. And the soul rejoices and is content. Paint me as I long to be and need to be and am.* This is the message of the graphic body. *Paint me brave. Paint me charming. Paint me clever, able, wise. Paint me eager to please but to mine own self true. Paint me human."*

For those who would like to know more about body paint-ing, I recommend the book, *Ritual Body Art - Drawing the Spirit*, by Charles Arnold, published by Phoenix Publishing Inc.

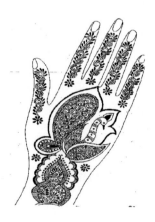

Celebrations

Celebrations as Ritual

"My name is Festivity. I am the daughter of Queen Celebration. We are guardians of all holidays. We bring diversion and distraction to those struggling with life. We put markers on the road of time, allowing for things past to be remembered. In measuring time, we give hope for things future. We guard the birthdays, anniversaries, and holidays that make a person particular. We are life's balancers. We are life's rhythm-makers."34

- Madeleine Pelner Cosman

"Celebrations" is assigned as the "miscellaneous" category of rituals. Included under the heading of celebrations are parades and processions, races and competitions, county fairs, birthdays, festivals, holidays, anniversaries, and other significant events that happen periodically in our lives. Cultural celebrations answer important questions about a society. "What did the people think beautiful? What was forbidden? What were the major sights of the daily life? The sounds? The tastes? The textures? The odors? What did the oldest people share with the youngest? What activities linked the most nobly born to the lowest? What was the people's ancient heritage? Did their culture cherish the past or reject it? What were the people's most important ideas? What was thought to be sacred? What did the people do for recreation?"35

Cultural celebrations unite a community in thought and action. Social status is equalled. All participants have the opportunity to play an important role in the celebration, during which, acceptable social information becomes integrated.

---

34. Cosman, Madeleine Pelner *Medieval Holidays and Festivals* page 3
35. Cosman, Madeleine Pelner *Medieval Holidays and Festivals* page 4

Races and Competitions

―――――――――――――――<　◆　>―――――――――――――――

The Olympics. The Kentucky Derby. The Indianapolis 500. World Cup Soccer. The World Series. The Superbowl. Wimbledon. The Iditarod. The Spelling Bee. Chinese Dragon Boat Races. Human beings have displayed physical, functional, technical, and tactical readiness in public competitions for centuries. Through training, breeding, planning and practicing, competitors gather to settle the ultimate question of superiority in full view of an audience. Spectators become involved in the competition as financial supporters, faithful fans, and cheering sections. A sense of pride or disappointment will be shared by competitor and community alike.

Elements of ritual are contained within each competitive event. There are starting lines and winner's circles, victory laps, half-time entertainment, parades, betting, victory celebrations, trophies, and medals. Oftentimes the races themselves are rich with symbolism and ritual. For example, the Chinese dragon boat races contain a ritual called the "Awakening of the Dragon" where the eyes of the dragon's head on each boat are dotted so as to cleanse and bless the area of the competition, the competitors and their boats. The dragon boat races initiated as a way to ensure prosperous and bountiful crops. Sumo wrestlers undergo an elaborate ceremony before the actual wrestling match occurs. Pure dirt is used to create the wrestling arena, which is then blessed and purified with salt. The wrestlers display a ritual exhibition of pounding the floor with their fists and staring each other down. All of this action occurs before the wrestling actually begins.

Races, such as the Iditarod Trail Sled Dog Race, commemorate a moment in cultural history. In 1925, the town of Nome, Alaska was engulfed in a diphtheria epidemic. The only way to get much-needed serum to the town was by dog sled. Twenty teams raced from Nenana, Alaska, to Nome, relaying the medicine a total of 674 miles in 127.5 hours. Today, the dogs race 1,200 miles between Anchorage and Nome Alaska, over a period of 10 to 12 days. Red lanterns still hang at the finish line as a memorial to similar lanterns used along old sled dog routes to help mushers find their way and to let people know that there were mushers on the trail.

Races, such as the Kinetic Sculpture Race in California, began in 1969 when Ferndale artist Hobart Brown, decided to make his son's tricycle look a little more interesting. Dubbed the 'Pentacycle", this five-wheeled creation was tall, wobbly, bright red and quite laughable - especially to other local artists who decided to build better "machines" and race them down Main Street, Ferndale, California. Kinetic Sculptures are human powered works of art designed to travel over all terrain (roads, sands, mud and water) in a highly sophisticated race which itself is a work of art. The sculptures must pose no threat of harm to its pilots or the world. The racer may use any materials in constructing the sculpture, and any concept on locomotion - so long as it is human powered. The race grew from a one-day event to the current tradition of a three-day race, which is celebrated today.

Parades and Processions

The celebration of national holidays or commemorative events is usually proceeded by a parade. The parade or procession provides a visual tutorial of the commemoration. Members of select groups within a community demonstrate, through exhibition, the meaning of the current event. In the midst of the parade itself are specific display rules and competitions which all participants become involved in.

Many parades trace their beginnings to an original "public statement" to society. In New York, the Macy's Thanksgiving Day parade can trace its beginnings to first generation immigrant employees who wanted to celebrate an American holiday in European tradition. "Coming Out" or Gay Pride parades display to the public that these people are not willing to hide themselves any longer. Mardi Gras parades in New Orleans can trace their history to European celebrations, which were transplanted in the New World.

One cannot mention parades and processions without mentioning the government. Oftentimes, military parades are symbolic displays of military victory or remembrance of past battles. Air shows demonstrate competitive pride, technology, and expertise to their audience. Military parades honor past or present veterans, display military prowess, or show support for current military policy. Political parades show support of political candidates, political parties and political policies. They set the tone for public opinion, and often reflect the public's response.

County Fairs

Another yearly ritual involving members of a community is the county fair. Once a year, residents of a town, county or large community exhibit and sell farm, agricultural, and manufactured products. Competitions of creativity and beauty, and various forms of entertainment often accompany the county fair. Local government officials often set the tone or theme for the community to focus on during the fair.

When county fairs first began in the 1800's, country folk and townsfolk traveled by wagons, buggies, horseback and on foot to attend the fair. Exhibitions were set up to enhance the county's image. Awards were given for competitions of livestock breeding, agricultural prowess and artistic expression. Local government and community leaders gave speeches. Entertainment, dancing, games and races were part of the festivities. The people stayed all day, into the night, and everyone brought their dinners with them.

The enormous size of modern county fairs requires a year-long dedication of planning, registration, and coordination. The location of the county fair is now fixed. Exhibit halls, food stands, grandstands, racetracks, show rings and stables have been constructed to house various exhibits. Social messages are still built into the theme of each fair. Livestock and agricultural competitions are still included. The commercial aspect of buying and selling arts and crafts has become a profitable industry within the constructs of the county fair.

The face of the county fair has changed over the years. Population and technology have changed the intimate nature of the county fair. Exhibitors and spectators are no longer known to each other. Brand-name artists often provide entertainment in order to attract revenue to the fair. And yet, the basic emphasis of providing a local event to connect the community with social, intellectual, and artistic commonality is still preserved through the planning of events, exhibits and entertainment for community participation.

Holidays

Thanksgiving. Memorial Day. Arbor Day. Labor Day. Easter. Mother's Day. Father's Day. Passover. Ramadan. Independence Day. Holy days. A day set aside by law or custom for the suspension of labor or business, usually in commemoration of some event. Every society gathers together its members for the collective remembrance of unifying events. Holidays are not necessarily celebrated for religious reasons. Often times, national holidays are in remembrance of significant moments of historical importance such as political independence, birthdays of honored leaders, in memorial of tragic occurrences, or to honor the community's hope for the future.

Holidays are often celebrated with parades, feasting, gift giving, or some type of ritual remembrance. Symbolic eating or abstaining from particular foods set apart those who participate in the honoring of tradition. Marking one's body or wearing distinctive apparel also serves a similar purpose. Those who celebrate holidays re-enact in some way the original event through the actions of the observance. Social or religious history is passed on through celebrations. Cultural thought and action becomes unified by the stopping of day-to-day activities to focus on a common event.

Birthday Celebrations

When we celebrate a birthday, we re-enact the original birth ceremony. The mother may be honored for bringing the child into the world, or the child may be honored for progressing to the current stage in his or her life. As an adult, birthday celebrations become a time of reflection of the life that he or she has lived so far. Gifts, parties, feasting, and birthday cards, are often ways that someone's day of birth is celebrated. Some adults choose to celebrate their birthday in solitude and reflection, some enjoy a public celebration with friends and family.

Solitary Birthday Celebration: Many, who choose to celebrate their birthday alone, do so in reflection of the meaning that their life has brought to the world. Contemplation of the events surrounding ones birth, re-imaging the birth circumstances as a welcoming celebration, reflecting on life's journey so far, the ebb and flow of the many years past, the circumstances of the present, and limiting patterns to release in the coming year. Solitary birthday celebrations are held in places that contain special meaning to the celebrant. Here is an example of a solitary birthday ceremony held by the ocean. It is a guided meditation containing a blessing, a call to the directions, and a rebirth of the soul, which is then connected to the adult being.

> Self Blessing
> I stand on the shore
> At the place of my birth.
> In the center of the circle I stand.
> My sweet grass smoking
> My feather gathering smoke
> To bless my spirit.
>
> Call to the Directions
> In the crash of a wave
> I call to the North and
> Ask for the blessings of
> Winter wisdom.

In the crash of a wave
I call to the South and
Ask for the blessings of
Innocence and trust.
In the crash of a wave
I call to the West and
Ask for the blessings of
Inner change.
In the crash of a wave
I call to the East and
Ask for the blessings of
Vision, illumination, and clarity.

Rebirth of the Soul
Within the sound of these blessings
From the four directions of the wheel
In smoke and in salt spray,
I hold the newborn soul.
I cradle her high in the moist wind
She drinks her first breath
Fills her lungs with the blessings
Of the directions uttering her first sound
Into the world and into the wind.
The wind swirls with each fragment
Of sound to the goddesses
Who in turn, gather the fragments
Of their echoes.
The soul child is lowered
To the earth circle
Mother Earth cradles her child
Her solid strength a foundation
Mother Ocean and the four winds
In turn sing their song of comfort
And universal knowledge.

The soul child is ready to journey
Another year.
I gather her to my root
  She resides in grounded strength

I gather her to my flower
  She resides in creative sensuality
I gather her to my solar plexus
  She resides in stamina and power
I gather her to my heart
  She resides in love and compassion
I gather her to my throat
  We speak in truth.
I gather her to my forehead
  We breathe in intuition
I gather her to my crown
  We follow the spirit threads that connect all.

We are one.
We are new
Never before and without end.
Added to.
Complete as one.
Ready to journey another year.

Public Birthday Celebrations: Public celebrations can be wild and exciting or a small gathering of intimate friendship. It is a time to play with friends, dance, share laughter, loyalty, thoughtfulness and caring. Publicly sharing one's birthday allows others to reflect qualities that the celebrant may not be aware of. In large celebrations the birthday person is "roasted," where participants share funny or embarrassing stories as well as sharing feelings about the person's quality of character. Another way to celebrate the character of the birthday person is to create a birthday scrapbook in which all party members contribute fond memories of how this person has touched their life. The birthday person gets to keep the scrapbook in remembrance of their birthday.

Anniversaries

Anniversaries are celebrated as the annual recurrence of the date of an earlier event. Anniversaries often carry special meaning to a smaller group of individuals: family members, workers, religious groups, social groups, and sole persons. Many people may recognize the date of a particular event, like the assassination of John F. Kennedy, or only a few may honor an anniversary, such as that of a family remembering a wedding date. Personal anniversaries such as the start of a business, the stopping of an addiction, or the beginning of a new career may be honored as a means to continue on when times seem to get rough. When life has moved on past the point of an important event, remembrance gives meaning to the life lived after the event. Anniversaries are often the marking of time past an event, a time to reflect back on how the particular event shaped people's lives.

Festivals

Festivals are joyful celebrations of a particular theme held periodically. Particular entertainment or a series of performances of a certain kind, such as a Shakespeare or Bach festival, focus on one theme. Farming communities hold festivals based on the particular agricultural product that the town is famous for, such as a strawberry or garlic festival, thereby promoting a social pride and commercial trade in the region. Ethnic groups may hold festivals as a way to honor their ethnic origins and as a cultural exchange with the surrounding community. Food, dance, and traditional entertainment are provided as a means of keeping their heritage alive in new environment.

Part 2:
Sample Rituals

Daily Rituals

Daily Rituals

The alarm rings and a new day begins. Do you pray first, grab a cup of coffee, read the paper, get the kids off to school, smoke, meditate, or rush to get yourself ready? Do you drive the same route, each lunch in a certain place or have special meals on specific days? Many of us greet each day without thinking, content in our routines. What happens after our eyes open each day can be a matter of choice or chance.

Morning Rituals

―――――――――――――――――――――⟪◆⟫――――――――――――――――

Upon waking,
The light of fire cuts through my curtains
To remind me
That there is so much more to life
Than what hides behind windows.

While I need rest, the world does not.
The stars are busy placing themselves
Neatly back on the shelves
Of heaven's darkness,
While the sun adjusts her costume
Before taking her place on stage.
Clouds swim constantly
In whatever colored skies,
Moisture inhales in evaporation,
Sighs in the ecstasy of falling
Back down to breathe in once again.

Rest, I must,
Because I am human.
Upon waking, I greet a world
That never sleeps.

Morning Devotions: We begin our day as if merging into flowing traffic. Our morning devotions are prayers and meditations. We "center up so we can stumble gracefully through the rest of the day." We ask for divine guidance, focus, protection and care. We honor and acknowledge all that is, and the source by which it exists. We do not have to "jolt" ourselves awake (caffeine, sugar) to be able to meet our day. We are able to trust in our connection to a more stable source of power.

Cleansing: The luxury of warm, flowing water refreshes our spirit. We are not only removing dead skin cells or dirt, but also re-baptizing the vessel of our soul, beginning this day as if it was our first. The pelting water awakens our sense of touch; our sense of smell is awakened by the fragrances of soap and shampoo. We remove all traces of yesterday's adventure and prepare ourselves for the wisdom of today.

Feeding: "Taking food into the body is a ritual way of absorbing the god into oneself...All eating is communion, feeding the soul as well as the body."36 The joy of ingesting culinary delights awakens our sense of taste, allowing us to experience a simple joy before work. Breakfast. The first meal of the day. Meant to "break" the "fast."

Dressing: The language of clothing can be a statement of authenticity, or the costume of our acting. Children play "dress up" to assume the identity that clothing offers. Many jobs require certain attire: hard hats, suits, uniforms, steel-toed boots, lap top, briefcase, phone. We step into our "work clothes" to assume the role of our profession, to become walking symbols of what we do.

---

36. Moore, Thomas *Care of the Soul* page 205

Mid-Day Rituals

As this day wears on
I feel my energy running low.
I fret, I doubt, I worry:
Will I be able to continue on,
How can I right the defects
In the work which I have begun?

Resting: Our lunch hours tend to be used as another space to fill with errands, meetings, appointments and negotiations instead of using it as a time to replenish our inner resources. Utilize this space (block) of time as the resting period that it was meant to be. Listen to calming music, breathe fresh air, take a nap, watch the clouds move across the sky, feel the elements on your face, experience natural light.

Mid-Day Prayers: Prayers and meditation at this time of the day are meant to reconnect us to the Spirit. Other "powers" may have eased their way into our minds (deadlines, authorities, setbacks, and crises). We need to find our way back to the true source of power. We need to regroup, refocus, and remember.

Eating: As well as becoming spiritually depleted, our bodies become drained of energy during the day. We need to refuel, and not with low octane. "Our cultural habit of eating 'fast food' reflects our current belief that all we need to take into ourselves, both literally and figuratively, is plain food, not food of real substance and not the imagination of real dining."37 Dining may include one or more of these qualities: the company of friendship, atmosphere, sumptuous food, or beautiful surroundings.

[37.] Moore, Thomas *Care of the Soul* page 205

Evening Rituals

---⟨◆⟩---

Noise diminishes into lullabies played on a harp.
Activity decreases to occasional stutters.
Daylight fades like an echo.
I end this day as I began,
In solitary reflection.

Dining: Dining is a ritual unto itself. Food is prepared with the main ingredient of the spirit of the cook. The table setting, like our bodies, is a vessel set to contain the artistic display of nourishment for our consumption. There is no half full/half empty glass, only the magnificent glass itself. We purify ourselves before sitting down to the table, removing from our hands any impediments to spiritual fulfillment. We ask a blessing on the food by saying "grace." By spiritual definition, "grace" is the divine boost we receive once we reach the end of our human limitation. When we eat, we are truly "absorbing the god into oneself."

Reflection: We cannot break the insanity of repeating patterns without awareness. We cannot move into tomorrow without lying to rest the weight of today. We cannot achieve awareness without reflection. Evening is the time in which we need to take inventory of our day. We reflect upon the events of today, looking at our actions and reflecting upon our feelings.

Prayer: As the day begins, so shall it end. Fresh with awareness, we communicate one more time with the Spirit. In doing so, we turn the events of each day into teachings from which we obtain wisdom. Doubt turns into assurance. Fragments of pain turn into the wholeness of gratitude and acceptance. You are now ready for the boundless world of dreams where you will work out the deeper issues of your being. Pray for guidance and protection. Pray for those with whom you have resentments. Be thankful for this one glorious day.

Spokes of the Wheel: Monthly Rituals

January Rituals

Ritual for the New Year

Counting down the seconds from one year to the next, we usher in the New Year with a gala celebration. We celebrate with music, food, dance, drink, party hats, confetti, noisemakers, stunning attire, and a kiss. Without any reflection of the past year's journey, we make our New Year's resolutions like promises meant to be broken.

This year we are going to create a Spirit Journal - a place to reflect and record the daily journey of our lives. This journal will hold the teachings you receive; your dreams, feelings, memories, drawings, quotes, questions, processes and miracles. The Spirit Journal will carry everything that holds meaning to you, everything that you experience, allowing you to make sense of what you see each day.

You may prefer to hold this ceremony alone, as a family ritual or in a group setting. It is a loosely structured ceremony due to the project of creating the Spirit Journal.

Preparation:

1. Think back to the beginning of the year (look at your journal, letters, and cards). Write a list of the questions, troubles, and events that were going on in your life. What were your issues? What did you accomplish? What moments brought you joy? How did you grow? What changes occurred in your life?

2. Find the materials for your journal. You may purchase a journal with a picture on the cover that seems to reflect who you are, or you may purchase articles from the materials list in this book. Purchase a special pen to keep with your journal.

Materials:

A notebook : colored, blank or lined paper and a good pen.
Cover material: leather, cloth, wrapping paper, colored paper, wood or cardboard with holes.
Decorations: glitter, feathers, pictures from magazines, beads,

sequins, paints, crayons, etc.

Miscellaneous: scissors, glue, ribbon, string, yarn, sage or sweet grass, a large feather, music, candles and incense.

Introduction:

At the end of December
Thinking of a New Year;
The time has come.
I began this year with loneliness and fear.
The loneliness is not as strong,
The fear is just about gone.
Stepping out of the shadows of a doorway,
Is a warrior maiden.
She has passed the winding test of
One year's dark labyrinth.
It is time to begin again,
To step through the keyhole doorway
Into the light of a new day,
Time to take the sword from the crone
And begin a new adventure.

Invocation/Purification:

Invite Spirit to be with you by offering a prayer. Include all of the directions: north, south, east, west, above, below, and within. Light a candle, for each direction, as the prayer is being offered.

Place a small amount of sage or sweet grass in a bowl and light it with a match. Blow out the flame. Gently blow (breath of life) on the embers to enhance the smoke.

Using the large feather, fan the smoke around your body (solitary ritual) or around the body of the person sitting next to you in the group. Fan the smoke over all of the materials to be used in creating your Spirit Journal.

Ceremony:

1. Open the New Year ritual by reviewing what you have written about the past year (solitary). Share the things that you have written with members of the group.

2. With music playing in the background, begin construction of your spirit journal. You may use pages of various

meaningful colors, personalize the cover with wrapping paper, glitter, paint, or pictures. You may write words of identification with the picture on the cover, a message of encouragement to your inner most self, or a quote you wish to remember.

3. Dedicate your journal. Be grateful for all you have experienced during the past year and ask for the blessing of courage, openness, willingness, and protection for the coming year.

4. If this is a group ceremony, share the special dedication of your journal with one another.

Closing:
      Close the ritual by thanking and releasing the Spirits who were in attendance during this ceremony.
      Have each person repeat these words: "There are no resolutions, only daily experiences. I ask for awareness and guidance each day of the New Year."

Ritual of Solitude

Amongst the revelry of daily activity
A pause, quite unexpected,
Yet, once savored by experience
Sought after with zeal;
It is then that the mischievous universe
Plays a game of tag with time.

Fancy clothing is put away. Echoes of festivity fade to silence. Time to pick up the old routine. Calendar days are no longer outlined in red or bold. A let down of sorts. A quieting. Snowfall is just winter. Rainy days are endless. We have received a new gift. The packaging is different. We are receiving solitude.

There is a gift that you didn't open this holiday season. The gift of solitude. This ritual is just for you.

Preparation:

1. Determine five places of solitude - real or imagined. For you, it could be at the beach, camping, your favorite park, a sunny spot in the backyard, your bedroom, the bathtub, the garage, or a cafe.

2. What is the atmosphere like? Sunshine, incense, music, absolute silence, floral arrangements, birds singing, a certain day of the week, etc.

3. How long will you devote to this solitude? Is 15 minutes enough? Is it an hour every morning? Is it a one-week pilgrimage a year?

4. What are your activities? Are you reading a book at a cafe while sipping your favorite beverage? Are you hiking in the woods and listening to the sounds of nature? Are you sitting in a bathtub filled with bubbles or oil, with the lights off and candles glowing?

<u>Materials</u>:
Yourself
Anything, you determined from your preparation, to provide an atmosphere of solitude.

<u>Invocation</u>:
I call upon the Power of my choosing to attend me during this ceremony of solitude. Awaken my spirit to all that is within me. Enlarge my soul to all that is around me. Be present while I learn how to Be.

You may wish to anoint yourself with scented oil, smudge yourself with sage or some other act of purification to mark the occasion as a sacred event. The point is to create an awareness of the choice of solitude, which is different than the pain of isolation.

<u>Ceremony</u>:
Silence has a voice of her own.
She speaks in a lace as delicate and strong
As a cobweb is to you and I or a fly.
In silence, colors sing.
Not only in association with being,
But of the secret melody of partnership
Between themselves and sound
Or taste
Or even scent.

Can you hear Silence sing in a dance of ¾ time?
How many continuous moments does it take
To smell green in all of it's shades?

Silence speaks where words dare not tell.
She does not require a communications planner,
Only the medium of her voice,
And the translation of Spirit.

Solitude is living or acting without others. Due to the fact that solitude can mean so many different things to different people, you must create the meat of this ceremony. Here are some suggestions to work with:

103

Listening to good music. Find music that you truly enjoy. Whether you listen under headphones or your stereo, listen to each instrument, sing with the lyrics as if you are the actual singer, imagine yourself creating a video, play "air guitar," or choreograph a dance.

People watching. Benches in the park or in a mall are excellent places to watch people. Really look at how human beings are constructed, notice the variety of the shape of noses, and watch how people walk. Who has the most outrageous outfit, who looks confident, what are the children doing?

Browsing in bookstores. A bookstore can be an affirming celebration of solitude. Books are so personal. They are an exchange of energy. A book cover catches your attention. Draws you in. Do you sit on the floor of the aisle to peruse its contents? Are there new categories to investigate? What about the "children's" section? Maybe you would like to explore books about art. Even though you do not have a "green thumb," books about gardening look beautiful to you.

Beach-combing. The calming sound of wave after wave. Consistency in a fast-paced environment. The ocean deposits her treasures along the shore. Hidden in the seaweed is a complete sand dollar. A rock, worn smooth by the waves, fits perfectly in the palm of your hand - like it was made just for you. A piece of driftwood, not very large, ocean salts and the sun has faded the color. Birds fly overhead. A moist wind blows in from the sea. Body and spirit absorb the scene.

Bubble bath. Evening time. In the midst of the cool darkness, a warm, fragrant luxury. The flickering of dancing candlelight breaks the dark. Meditative music echoes in the acoustically perfect, tiled room. There you are in the midst of it all. Treating yourself, as you have always wanted to be treated. Thoughts ramble aimlessly through your mind, and if you choose to, you may stop one or two of them to explore their possibilities.

Fishing. When I was a child, fishing was not so much about catching fish as it was about daydreaming. The boat, the equipment, the water lapping against the sides of the boat or sloshing against your legs...waiting for the fish. Imagine the underwater universe.

So foreign. The sky reflects itself on the face of the water; bugs defy gravity by skating along the surface.

Creative endeavors. Painting a picture, experimenting with a new recipe, beading, quilting, machining, making a model, playing an instrument, etc. The world disappears. All that remains is the project and you. Color, sight, sound, smell, touch, taste - they all take on new meaning. You begin to notice the effect of space, how colors harmonize with one another, the blending of ingredients creating a whole new sensation. You experience rhythm; the rhythm of movement, the pulse of the world around you, your own heartbeat, and the heartbeat of the medium with which you are connected to.

Closing:

      After your ceremony of solitude is complete, it is time to ease yourself back into the world. Bring a memento of the ceremony home with you. Write the experience in a journal, bring a shell home from the ocean, hang your masterpiece, etc. Release the Spirit that attended you during the ceremony. Thank it for the gift of a moment of serenity.

February Rituals

Ritual of Patience

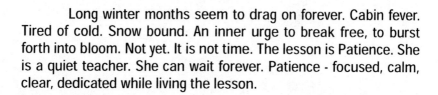

Long winter months seem to drag on forever. Cabin fever. Tired of cold. Snow bound. An inner urge to break free, to burst forth into bloom. Not yet. It is not time. The lesson is Patience. She is a quiet teacher. She can wait forever. Patience - focused, calm, clear, dedicated while living the lesson.

Materials:
White candles
Sage or sweet grass

Invocation/Purification:
> In this circle we gather.
> We ask for blessings of openness and willingness.
> We are thankful for the lessons of the process.
> Help us to understand the wisdom of patience.
>
> We light the candle of understanding.
> We are not alone as we travel this journey.
> We purify one another with the smoke of sage.
> We clear our minds and hearts of fear.

Ceremony:
Release all other light from the room except for the light of the white candles.

Close your eyes. Breathe in and out. With every exhalation, let go of fear, tension and stress. With every inhalation, breathe in the love of the universe. Relax your body. Feel yourself touching the floor. Let go.

As you relax, you begin to see a car. This is not just any car, but your favorite. The car that you have always wanted. This car is fast, it handles like a dream, and there are no limitations. You get into the car, the gas tank is full, the road before you is empty. Drive any way that you like on this road, there are no speed limits. Feel the sensation of power and speed, feel the freedom from limitations.

Now, begin to notice other cars driving along the same road. There is a traffic jam. You have to slow down to stop-and-go traffic. You grow tired, irritated. Is there somewhere that you needed to be? Do you feel trapped? Are you thinking of other routes that you could have traveled? Do you want to yell at another driver for moving so slow? Do you scan the radio for reports of an accident?

Remember to relax once again. Focus on breathing slowly. Breathe deep. Breathe in and out. Feel yourself sitting on the seat of the car. Patience is the key. Look around. Did you miss those flowers growing along the side of the road? Did you miss the clouds or the music on the radio? Maybe you brought a friend with you to talk to. It is acceptable to slow down. You have plenty of time. Look at the others who are irritated and shouting. You are not one of them. Practice. This is only practice. The outcome will be acceptable.

When you are ready, feel your body on the floor, feel your breath flowing in and out, and open your eyes. One at a time, share your experience of the guided meditation with the group.

Closing:
We release the guidance of the Spirit and carry with us the teachings from Patience. We know that eventually the situation will change. Until it does, we can be content. We are not pushed and pulled by a lack of understanding.

Ritual for A Rainy Day

Staring out of the window. Just sitting and staring. Does it matter if the rain is real or if it just feels like a rainy day? Maybe you do not feel like doing something structured, but doing nothing feels a bit overwhelming. The sun could be shining but you do not see it. Stress fills your mind with too many problems. That empty kind of feeling has invaded your body. Some people call it being off-center or feeling blue. Maybe the internal vocal committee is staging a riot in your head. What do you need to do? Return to the land of your soul.

Preparation:
1. Somewhere in your home, create a sacred space. Place blankets and pillows on the floor.
2. Find background music that contains no words.
3. Make popcorn or other finger snacks.

Materials:
Hot chocolate, tea, or something luxurious to sip
Popcorn
Potpourri, essence oils, incense, or sage
Candles
Blankets and pillows
Loose, comfortable clothes
Music with no words
Paper, crayons, magazines, colored pens, tape, glue, and scissors

Purification/Invocation:
Fill the room with your favorite potpourri, essence oils, incense, or sage. Light candles to add to the calming atmosphere. Take a moment to connect with the Spiritual Power of your choice. Set the intention for your actions by holding a question, phrase or statement in your mind.

A picture has the nerve to say
The thing that words dare not...

Because a picture tends to say a thousand words, your ritual will use images to unlock what cannot be said with words. Rainy-day emptiness is often a disconnection with our spirit. This ritual is meant to draw from the inner sunshine of our souls.

Shadow venting. Fill a page with words that you would never say or actions you would not take. Become daring. Find pictures and phrases, which reflect aspects of yourself that you are not comfortable with. Roam through the images freely without restrictions or consequences.

Theme collage. If you cannot think of a theme then let the theme be anything that catches your eye in a magazine. Cut out the pictures and paste or tape them onto your paper. By the time you are finished, a common thread may appear.

Doodle journal. Draw stick figure scenes. Remember that you are not being graded on artistic ability. Put labels next to the drawings. Use the crayons to create color doodles of feelings. Release them on paper.

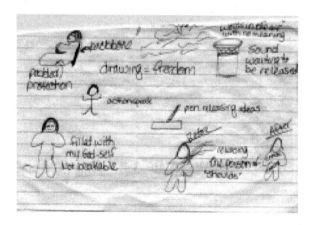

March Rituals

Joy in Spite of Difficulty

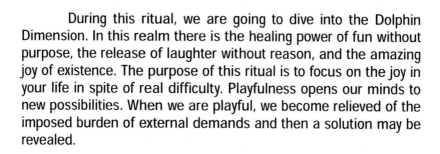

During this ritual, we are going to dive into the Dolphin Dimension. In this realm there is the healing power of fun without purpose, the release of laughter without reason, and the amazing joy of existence. The purpose of this ritual is to focus on the joy in your life in spite of real difficulty. Playfulness opens our minds to new possibilities. When we are playful, we become relieved of the imposed burden of external demands and then a solution may be revealed.

Materials:
Gardenia or water-lilies
Orange essence oil
Candles: Turquoise blue, green, violet, white-gray
Dolphin pictures or figurines
Meditation music: related to dolphins

Invocation:
We invite into our midst the playful spirit of the dolphin.
Our hearts may be full at this moment, but there is much more to our lives than the burdens that we carry.
Remind us of the vastness of our Mother Ocean.
Show us how to glide through the water, how to leap amongst the waves; take us to the heart of joy.

Purification:
Purify the person next to you with a drop of orange essence oil. Say the words "You are a dolphin at play."

Ceremony:
Play the meditation music. Have everyone sit comfortably.
Release all light from the room except for the light of the candles.

Close your eyes. Breathe in and out. Inhale and exhale in long, slow breaths. With every exhalation, let go of burdens, tension and stress. With every inhalation, breathe in the love of the universe. Relax your body as if it were floating in water.

As you continue to relax, focus your attention on the image of a dolphin. Imagine yourself swimming among playful friends in the vast blue ocean. Your motions are almost effortless. Your dolphin body moves freely through the water. A game begins. It is one of leaping high into the air. You hear yourself laugh as you leap and spin in the air. Your landing in the water creates a large splash. Or maybe you arch gracefully and dive back into the sea. Your concerns are far away. The concerns of the entire ocean are not yours to carry. Your presence reflects the joy of living. You gather the Divine breath from the surface and carry it to your home below. The Divine breath is filled with excitement and joy. Your whole being radiates with happiness.

When you are ready, feel your body on the floor, feel your breath flowing in and out, and open your eyes. One at a time, share your experience of the guided meditation with the group.

<u>Closing</u>:
We release the playful dolphin spirit from our circle. May we keep in our hearts the focus of joy and playfulness no matter what our external circumstances are.

Renewal Ritual

During this month we glimpse the struggle for rebirth. One day a blinding blizzard covers the earth. The next week, temperatures soar. Windows open and then close. Jackets are removed and then we have to bundle up. Renewal comes in fits and starts. The energy builds. Nature is waking and stretching. Her palate is covered in waiting colors.

Preparation:

1. Dye the eggs with commercial or natural dyes.
2. Remove the whites and yolks from uncooked eggs by carefully piercing (perforating) the shell with a pin.
3. Fill several small bowls with small materials to place inside of the eggs: confetti, potpourri, glitter, etc.
4. Prepare an altar with baskets or vases of flowers for the four directions, and green candles.

Materials:

East: white flowers (daisies, lilies)
South: yellow, orange or red flowers (daffodils)
West: blue flowers or water plants (hyacinth, water lilies)
North: greens (ivy, herbs)
Green candles
Prepared eggs
Bowl of salted water for purification
Pieces of paper (to write on) and pencils
Colored markers
Tape

Invocation:

We call to this circle the Spirit of Spring. We invite the presence of playfulness and open hearts. In the spring we honor the dawn, the rising sun, and the renewal of life. We call to the directions and honor their floral representations.

Purification:

Dip your fingers in the bowl of salted water. Anoint the fore-head of the person sitting next to you and say the words, "I awaken your sleeping dreams."

Introduction:
Within the egg of Mother Earth lies the potential for new life. Beneath Her strong but fragile shell, lies the symbol of fertility, and the symbol of the life-giving sun reflected in Her yolk. Beneath our own strong but fragile shell, dreams begin to stir. Restless, they push against our boundaries, gaining the strength to emerge.
Spring is about beginnings. Beginnings are new opportuni-ties. Beginnings are as fragile as the shell of an egg. Beginnings develop in the dark within. Beginnings may contain hundreds of failed attempts before gaining their own momentum. Once begin-nings finally take hold, they have their own power and energy.

Ritual:
1.Write down on the small pieces of paper, dreams that you wish to have awakened.
2.Fold the pieces of paper into a small enough size to fit into the empty eggs.
3.Carefully fill the empty eggs with confetti, potpourri, flower petals, and your written dreams. Place tape over the opening.
4.Let each participant light the person's candle sitting next to them.
5.Begin to chant quietly and grow louder with each repeti-tion:

By the fire of the sun
By the warmth of the fire
Let the sleeping dreams of this earth
Awaken!!!

6.Gently have one of the participants break your egg open over your head, pouring over you the playfulness of spring and the awakening of your dreams.

Closing:

Close the ceremony by thanking and releasing the Spirits and the directions. End the ceremony with feasting.

April Rituals

Spring Cleaning Ritual

As the sun begins to shine warmth into the atmosphere, a sweet fragrance replaces the closed, musty air of the past months. Nature opens, stretches, blossoms, brings forth, ventures out, and replenishes the world with color, scent and population. It is time for us to offer our homes the same gift that nature offers the earth - a spring-cleaning. This is the time to put up window screens, plant seeds and bulbs, put heavy clothing into storage, and air out the stale atmosphere of winter from our homes.

Preparation:
> 1. Find lively music to play in the background while you work.
> 2. Divide the tasks according to ability. Leave the more difficult tasks as a group effort.
> 3. Make sure that you have all cleaning, repair, and gardening supplies on hand.
> 4. Select a warm sunny day for this ritual.

Materials:
Cleaning, repair and gardening supplies
Lively music
Celebration treat (fresh salad, juice)

Prayer:
> The sleep of winter has passed.
> Our hibernation within is complete.
> Bless us as we prepare our home
> For the activity of the coming months.
> Let us awaken the splendor of our home
> With the sights and scents of freshness.
> Let the beauty of our home reflect our own.

<u>Ceremony</u>:

Fresh from the morning shower
Nature has cleansed our Mother Earth,
Washed away from her face the darkness.
She stretches green from the dream
Welcoming multitudes
From their solitude
And silence.

We gather today to return to splendor the sacred space of our home. This home has sheltered our family from the cold and storms of winter months, it has protected us during our quiet growth, held feelings of joy and disappointment, holiday vacations, and sighs of someday plans. Today, we open our home to spring, to the rebirth of possibilities and beauty.

Hand out the task lists, letting each person know that they have the privilege of honoring the home with their special ability to complete each task that they are given. Play lively music to accompany your work. Let the spirit of springtime enter your home through attitude as well as accomplishment.

<u>Closing</u>:

Take a step back and admire the splendor of your home. Congratulate everyone for a job well done. Replenish your energy with fresh juice and salad.

Arbor Day Ritual

Trees have long held a certain kind of magic. Tales of haunted forests, wood nymphs, wooden limbs capturing trespassers, and the eerie sound of wind moving through branches have fascinated listeners on many a night. Trees have provided shade, fruits, nuts, fuel, oxygen, medicine, warmth and protection. Ancient peoples honored the fact that trees contributed to their survival. Today we carelessly wipe out entire forests without ceremony.

J. Sterling Morton founded Arbor Day in the once treeless state of Nebraska. Typically celebrated on the last Friday in April, this tree-planting holiday of the 1800's is more meaningful than ever today.

Preparation:

1. Many cities offer grants for the purchase of trees. Volunteers, schools, or other organizations are encouraged to take the trees and plant them in designated areas.

2. Have children create and display artwork or poetry on the theme of trees.

3. Investigate the possibility of "tree care" projects.

4. Determine a person or organization for which you would like to dedicate the tree as a living monument.

Materials:
Gardening supplies
Trees
Water (hose, or buckets)
Cornmeal, sage, or sweet grass

Invocation:

Ask for blessings on yourselves and on the materials to be used to plant the trees. Ask for the earth to be blessed in receiving the tree. Ask for a blessing on the water, that it will nourish the tree. Ask for blessings on the trees themselves, that they will grow healthy and strong. Thank the trees for supporting our needs.

Ceremony:

The selfishness of man
Would take what the earth has given,
Using without care.
Let us return in small measure,
A future for our today.

1. Determine where the tree will be planted. Dig a hole deep enough for the tree to be planted in.
2. Sprinkle cornmeal around the hole, creating a sacred circle for the tree to be planted in. Purify the ground through a combination of prayer or smudging with sage/ sweet grass.
3. Plant the tree into the sacred site.
4. Dedicate the tree as a living monument to a loved one or organization. A tree or bush could be planted for each child in the family, or in loving devotion to one who has passed on.

Closing:

Place a circle of stones, around the base of the tree, as a reminder of this ceremony. Revisit the tree on special occasions to mark new growth or seasonal changes.

May Rituals

Playing Dress-Up

The dreariness of winter has given way to color and warmth. Spring has awakened and put on a fashion show of blossoms, leaves, and brilliance. We can change our seasonal mood by playing dress-up. Playing dress-up can be an enriching indulgence to be savored alone or with accomplices. Dress-up can be as simple as "changing your look" with a shopping spree, or dressing different for one day and watching the response.

Preparation:
1. Make a list of personas: movie star, biker, model, pirate, etc.
2. Explore your closet, jewelry box, magazines, local consignment shop or thrift store.
3. Have participants bring dress-up components: shoes, jewelry, clothes, make up, hats, beauty supplies, wigs, fake mustaches or beards, eyelashes, scarves, corsets, boots, boas, etc.
4. Decide if you want this ritual to be based on a certain theme or an exploration of personalities.

Materials:
Dress-up paraphernalia in a pile
Camera
"Kid" snacks
Bubbles
Feathers
Sandalwood incense
Mirrors

Introduction:
Who are you today? Are you your authentic self? How do you know? Has your mood changed? Are you more daring, childlike, adventurous, sensual, sea faring, rodeo-riding, glamorous, professional, rowdy? Who would you secretly pretend to be?

<u>Purification</u>:
Light the sandalwood incense to purify the room.

To invite a spirit of playfulness for this ritual, have each person take a feather and tickle the face of the person next to him or her and say the words "let's play dress-up."

<u>Ceremony</u>:

It is amazing, how, on Halloween
You have permission to be yourself.
My official title for today:
"New Age, Metaphysical Goddess,"
And they buy it!

A dress that flows, jewelry of my choosing,
Hair wild, makeup defining,
A goddess amulet dangling from my neck,
Fragrant essence oils coating my skin.
Sensual. Alive.

Select items from the pile of dress-up paraphernalia. Help each other with make up, accessories and ideas. Look in the mirror. Play out your personas with acting and interacting. Have sword fights and tea parties. Take pictures of one another.

<u>Closing</u>:
Close with a feast of kid snacks and blowing bubbles.

Naming Ceremony

When a child arrives in the world we celebrate its existence by selecting a name by which they shall be known, a name to distinguish and celebrate this child's spirit.

This ceremony is to name the adult, to honor the qualities of spirit, to look past the outer frailties to the inner being. At the heart of this ceremony is a bonding of spirits; for once we recognize the good in one another, we can recognize it in ourselves. Once we recognize it in ourselves, we can begin to move freely amongst one another without fear.

The two books influenced this naming ceremony are, *A Wind in the Door*, by Madeleine L'Engle, and *Spirit Medicine*, by Wolf Moondance.

Preparation:

1. For background material, read the book *A Wind in the Door* by Madeleine L'Engle. This "children's" story depicts the importance of Naming one another. In the book *Spirit Medicine*, by Wolf Moondance, read pages 118 - 123.

2. Find books that contain the meaning and history of various names.

Many traditions base human names on the important social aspects of life. Some tribal names are based on aspects of natural spirit: animal, environmental, aquatic, universal. Some archaic names are based on mythological deities, saints or a personal characteristic in relationship to God. Think back to the name selections of the sixties.

Materials:

Black alter cloth
Yellow or gold candles
Bowl of salt water for purification
Sandalwood oil or incense
Drum or quiet drum music

Invocation:

> Let us join together, in this circle, like the infinite universe.
> We call upon Spirit to join us in this circle.
> We ask Spirit to open our eyes and hearts so that we may
> see the true essence of one another. We pray to receive a
> vision of wholeness.
> Let us not be blinded by fear and past pain, instead,
> Let us hear the song of the universe as it burns our hearts.
> Let us hear the distinct melody of one another.

Purification:

Light the sandalwood incense to purify the room.

Dip your fingers in the bowl of salt water. Anoint the forehead of the person sitting next to you and say the words, "I welcome you to this circle of love."

Introduction:

> *"You are given the name that you walk with in your spirit,*
> *For your name is your spirit...All names are the same*
> *All names are sacred.*
>
> *The voice is that of prayer.*
> *We pray for your name, for your inner spirit to come forth.*
> *There you will hold within you the name.*
> *You might be a Dream Keeper, one who holds dreams.*
> *You might be a Rainbow Maker, one who organizes dreams,*
> *Holding on for all they are worth, carrying them to the altar*
> *Each day and leaving them there with prayers.*
> *All of us hold names within us.*
> *They come forth in the circle of whispering."*[38]

Ceremony:

Release all other light from the room except for the light of

---

[38] Moondance, Wolf *Spirit Medicine* pages 118 - 123

the gold candles. Begin a soft beat on the drum - a heartbeat, a focusing point.

Close your eyes. Breathe in and out. With every exhalation, let go of fear, tension and stress. With every inhalation, breathe in the love of the universe. Relax your body. Focus on the sound of the drum. Feel yourself touching the floor. Let go.

As you relax, allow the heartbeat of the drum to carry your spirit. Move past your heart. Move past your mind. Move into your soul - into your vision of wholeness. You begin to feel a pull towards your inner home, where you are everything and everything is you. You hear a song. It is familiar. It is the music of your wholeness. It contains a dance of wind and flame, a swirling of freedom, melody and joy.

Among the black of the universe shines the brightness of a golden star. The star in its dance of joy and wholeness feels no restriction of position or distinction. The star is one among stars. The star has a name that is known by the whole universe. The name is _____.

The star travels near the earth. It begins to enter Earth's atmosphere and blazes in the glory of freedom, joy and naming. It chooses a body to enter. This body is your own. You contain the blazing glory of this star. You contain the song of the star. You contain the dance of joy and wholeness. You contain the name. You are the name. You are. Be.

When you are ready, feel your body on the floor, feel your breath flowing in and out, and open your eyes. One by one, share with the group your experience of the guided meditation.

Closing:
We release the guidance of the Spirit and carry with us the wholeness of our Naming. We are known throughout the universe. Our spirits dance in joy and wholeness. In this body we are able to move on this earth and sing the true melody of our songs.
Turn to the person next to you and say these words:
"(Their name)_____! You are Named! My arms surround you. You are no longer nothing. You are. You are filled. You are me. You are (your name)_____."

June Rituals

Hiking Ritual

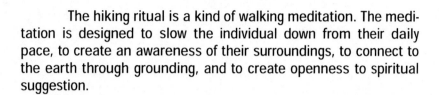

The hiking ritual is a kind of walking meditation. The meditation is designed to slow the individual down from their daily pace, to create an awareness of their surroundings, to connect to the earth through grounding, and to create openness to spiritual suggestion.

Preparation:
1. Select an area to hike in. There is no need to scale a mountain. Many state parks contain modest terrain for the novice hiker.
2. Consult with your doctor about your physical condition.
3. Plan the length of your hike. Is it only for a few hours or overnight? What supplies do you need?
4. Break in your hiking boots or walking shoes. A hike does not need to be painful.
5. Determine if this will be a solitary or group expedition.

Materials:
Hiking gear: boots, comfortable clothing, maps, water
overnight supplies (if necessary), tobacco, small seeds or grain,
a journal, sage or sweet grass

Invocation/Purification:
Invite Spirit to be with you by offering a prayer. Include all of the directions: north, south, east, west, above, below, and within. Ask for guidance and protection as you hike.

Place a small amount of sage or sweet grass in a bowl and light it with a match. Blow out the flame. Gently blow (breath of life) on the embers to enhance the smoke. Using the large feather, fan the smoke around your body (solitary ritual) or around the body of the person sitting next to you in the group. Fan the smoke over all of your hiking provisions.

<u>Ceremony</u>:

Every step we take
Caresses the face of Mother Earth.
She caresses our feet in return.
Footsteps -
Echoes of our soul.
Each footstep is a rhythm in the void.
Our presence is announced.
The universe is listening.

Mindfulness will be the key word during this hiking ritual. Be mindful of your footsteps. Feel every footstep as it connects with the earth. Be mindful of the earth's surface. Are you walking on gravel, pine needles, leaves, or soft earth? Relax your body as you walk, let your weight drop to your feet, let go of tension. Be mindful of the rhythm of your stride.

As your walking becomes grounded, become mindful of the information that your senses are picking up. Smell the fragrance of the air, listen for the scurrying of small animals or the flow of small streams, pick up leaves, acorns, or stones, smell flowers, or search for hidden trails.

Become mindful of your body, your breathing, tension, hunger, perspiration, fatigue, resistance, and exhilaration.

Become mindful of your thoughts, ideas and emotions. Are you processing or receiving? Is there a place along this trail that calls to you? Make a give-away to this sacred location. Honor the trees by leaving tobacco leaves. Honor the animals by leaving small seeds and grain.

<u>Closing</u>:

Record your experiences in your journal or share them with the other members of your group. When you leave, thank the Spirit and the trail for your experiences.

Midsummer Eve Ceremony

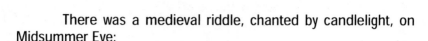

There was a medieval riddle, chanted by candlelight, on Midsummer Eve:

Green is Gold
Fire is Wet
Future's Told
Dragon's Met

Midsummer Eve is celebrated around the time of the summer solstice, usually June 23. It is a time of feasting, fortune telling, dancing and merrymaking for men and women. At this time of the year, in Europe, the young leaves looked golden. It was customary to float lighted candles, containing wishes, from one side to another of a pool of water. Fortunes were told with St. John's bread (carob), or St. John's wort, both named for John the Baptist whose birthday was said to be on Midsummer Day. Participants asked questions of the future beginning with the phrase "how many..." Then they bit into the bread and counted the number of seeds in one bite. To finish the festivities, one who is enacting the role of St. George must symbolically kill a huge dragon (usually a kite or pastry).

Preparation:

1. Create a birch wreath or garland made of small leaf branches or a sprig of new green leaves pinned to the left side of the chest, over the heart.
2. Buy or make pastry in the shape of a dragon.
3. Find a "pool" for the "wet fire" ritual (a water-filled tub, a children's play pool, etc.).
4. Create and cleanse a ceremonial space.

Materials:
Watermelon
Floating candles
Dragon-shaped pastry
Flowers, Blankets
Pool, or tub of water
Drums, rattles, bells, or other rhythm instruments

Purification:

As each participant enters the ceremonial space, either pin the sprig of green leaves over the left side of their chest, or place the wreath or garland on their head. Say the words, "Welcome to the enchantment of summer."

Invocation:

Set the intention for the ceremony. Honor the sacred space with the Spirit of your belief. Invite the spirit of joy and playfulness to awaken the Light within each participant.

Ceremony:

This is a loosely structured and fun event. If there is a large number of people in attendance, the ceremony may begin and end in one large group, while breaking up into smaller groups to participate in the activities.

Drum for at least 15 - 30 minutes to awaken the energy of the participants. Drum until reservations, embarrassment and thoughts from the everyday world are set aside.

Activities:

1. Wet fire ritual. Have each participant light a floating candle. Have them make a wish and set the candle into the "pool." When the candle reaches the other side, then their wish will come true.

2. Fortune telling. Have each participant ask a question which requires a numeric answer, i.e. how many, how much, how long, etc. When they bite into the watermelon, have them count the number of seeds and this will be the answer to their question. Or, the participants can play the "loves me, loves me not" game by removing the petals of a flower one at a time. With each alternating petal say the words he/she loves me or he/she loves me not.

3. Symbolically killing the dragon. Have each participant think of a character trait, feeling, memory, fear, belief system or any other fire-breathing "dragon" in their life. Have them "destroy" their dragon by slicing and eating a piece of the pastry and saying the words, "you will no longer threaten my kingdom."

When everyone has participated in the above activities,

132

gather everyone together for star watching.

Ask everyone to lie on his or her back and relax. Breathe deeply while looking up at the stars. See how the fiery energy of the stars pokes their way through the dark blanket of the night sky. Find a star that seems to be attracting you. Feel the energy of that star, hear its song, watch it dance. Reach your left hand to the sky and draw down the stellar energy. Let the energy flow through your hand into the rest of your body. Make a wish for yourselves and one for the rest of the world.

Closing:

When everyone is done gazing at the stars, close the ceremony with more drumming. Release the presence of any Spirits that had been called to the sacred space. Finish the celebration with feasting and dancing.

July Rituals

Family Reunion Ritual

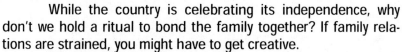

    While the country is celebrating its independence, why don't we hold a ritual to bond the family together? If family relations are strained, you might have to get creative.

    This ritual is loosely structured to allow for cultural, regional, or traditional differences. You may choose to base the family gathering on past family traditions or you may choose to create new ones of your own.

Preparation:

    1. Who are your "family" members? If circumstances have left you with no "family," create a "family of choice." Gather together with those who have stood by your side as family members.

    2. Begin a reunion fund. Family members can contribute funds to those who do not have the means to travel.

    3. Plan the family "event," the centering activity for the family members. Take into account, the age and ability of family members.

    4. Plan the location of this event. A park, meeting hall, your backyard, an amusement park - it all depends on the number of people who will attend and the planned activities. If family members are coming from out of town, where will they stay?

Opening:

    Depending on the circumstances, the family reunion might begin with a prayer, a meal, or a message from a family elder.

Announcements:

    When all of the family members have arrived, any changes or additions to the family can be announced. New members are made to feel welcome.

Activities:

1. If the family is large or spread out all over the country, a central meeting place may have been determined. Some families meet together at an amusement park (if there are many children or those who are young at heart), Las Vegas, camping at a national park, a rafting or fishing trip, volleyball at the beach, etc. After the major activities are over, the family could gather together for a meal before parting.

2. The family activity could be centered on the birthday of a patriarch or matriarch of the family. The event could be a potluck, house party, barbecue, or open house in which family members contribute food and honor an elder family member.

3. Family members could share events from their life. Select a theme for everyone to speak about "I remember when...," or "the funniest thing that happened was...," famous family members, infamous family members, immigration stories, survival stories, etc.

4. Select a family project to work on. Create a family quilt, plant a family garden, undertake a community project, add names to the family tree, etc.

Closing:
This depends on the family structure. A closing prayer might be offered, a final meal before everyone goes home, wishes for the safe return of traveling family members, a farewell at the airport. In general, thank everyone for attending and wish them well until you meet again.

Treasure-Hunt Ritual

A treasure-hunt ritual involves the following of clues to find a prized treasure in the end. It contains the classic aspects of growth to maturity, adventure to destiny, and anticipation to fulfillment. Elements of legend, competition, wit and mystery flavors the quest. Tales are passed on through generations of the heroes and heroines created from the adventure. Quiet, unobtrusive, misfits find the true nature of their spirit, and their thread in the fabric of time.

Preparation:

1. Create a "legend" about the hidden treasure. Are there pirates, mythological creatures, or interactions between mortals and deities? Why was it hidden? What is the treasure? What happened to the person who hid the treasure? Are there variations of the same story? Include "hints" and "clues" within the story.

2. Develop a "clue" list for the participants to follow. This could involve parts of a letter that need to be pieced together in order to solve the mystery, riddles hidden in various places, characteristics of an emotion, etc.

3. Draw a treasure map.

4. Make a treasure chest, with the "treasure" inside.

5. Decorate your ritual area with theme material related to your particular legend.

Materials:

Legend

Treasure chest

Costumes (if you wish to act out the scenes): pirates, medieval, fantasy world, etc.

Decorations (according to the type of legend)

Clue list

Treasure map

The following is a sample treasure-hunt ritual.

The first sounds that Gloria heard were that of running water and eerie music. She caught a glimpse of something glowing, a warm yellow light emanating from the very place where her mother had stopped to pray. Being a child, Gloria didn't think much about the glowing, the music or her mother's strange habit of singing and praying by the stream.

As Gloria grew older, she began to hear stories at school; fantastic stories about a crystal star falling to earth in the midst of the small town. The star shattered into many pieces as it struck the ground with tremendous force. The fallen star caused the townspeople to be afraid. Rumors, concerning the whereabouts of the fragments of the star began to circulate. Some of the townspeople began to believe that the star pieces contained great power, but no one was able to find such fragments – no one except Clara.

Clara was a young widow with one child; a little girl named Gloria. Rumor had it that Clara went about gathering the broken pieces of the crystal star. Each shard sang a song of emotional glory, of their blessed quality alone and as part of the whole. Each crystal was one note of a glorious song, and Clara would sing this song to herself day after day.

Gloria grew more interested in the world of her friends and spent less time in her mother's quiet world of odd behavior. Gloria scoffed at rumors and legends, distancing herself, closing the door tighter and tighter upon her home. Gloria wanted nothing to do with shattered crystal stars or the glowing beauty of her mother, or the silly music she made...until the day that her mother disappeared.

The sun shone directly overhead. To some, the bright flash of light was nothing more than the sun's reflection caught in a car mirror. No one could have known that Clara had collected enough of the crystal shards to complete the star, and with its completion, the creation of wholeness. Clara had vanished. She left behind a note to her daughter Gloria, a letter with clues to lead her to where the crystals were hidden.

Clue List:

The Qualities = *The Book of Qualities* by J. Ruth Gendler

The Wind = a blue bowl
Excitement = orange socks
Trust = door
Truth = altar
Commitment = balloons
Doubt = the living room (the treasure map is located here)

My Dearest Gloria,
The way of understanding the whole is first to understand The **Qualities** of her many facets. Finding the broken shards of the fallen star was the easy part. My first clue was to follow **The Wind**. I began to hear the song of the scattered shards and I was filled with **Excitement**.

I know how the townspeople were talking. I **Trusted** that you would one day learn the

Truth. I hope that you will **Commit** to the process of finding the crystals and becoming whole. Do not **Doubt** my love for you.
Love Mom

Treasure:
In the treasure chest have rocks or crystals with the various Qualities attached to them. Everyone is to reach in a take a rock or crystal, read the page associated with that particular quality and share how this quality creates contributes to the wholeness of their life.

Closing:
Everyone is to join hands in a circle. Turn the circle into a star by pointing one hand toward the center of the circle. When a star has been formed, say the words "by gathering the Qualities together, we have become whole."

August Rituals

Transforming Anger Ritual

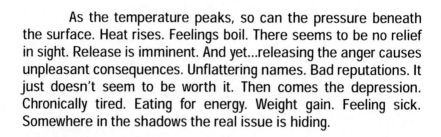

As the temperature peaks, so can the pressure beneath the surface. Heat rises. Feelings boil. There seems to be no relief in sight. Release is imminent. And yet...releasing the anger causes unpleasant consequences. Unflattering names. Bad reputations. It just doesn't seem to be worth it. Then comes the depression. Chronically tired. Eating for energy. Weight gain. Feeling sick. Somewhere in the shadows the real issue is hiding.

Preparation:
> 1.Arrange an altar or sacred space with the purple altar cloth, candles, stones, and symbols of the goddess Pele.
> 2.Have participants wear loose clothing, or something that they would feel comfortable moving around in.

Materials:
Ylang-ylang essential oil
Votive candles
Bright yellow and red stones
Symbols, pictures or figurines of the goddess Pele
Drums, rattles, percussion instruments
Cedar or sage
Feather fan
Purple altar cloth – promotes concentration

Invocation:
> From the direction of North we call to this circle the winds of spirit energy. From the land of death where endings signify the starting place for new beginnings, bring to this circle prayers of strength carried through the air.
> From the direction of South, we call to this circle the red-hot passion of summer. Sultry-sweat of energy expended; bring to this circle the purity of vital action.
> From the direction of East we call to this circle the spirit of the winged ones. Birds of fire, birds of regeneration, bring to this circle the spewing flames of a new beginning.
> From the direction of West, we call to this circle the intro-

spective spirit hidden beneath the earth. From your world of dreams the truth is buried. Bring to this circle the banished power that has been forced to live beneath the surface.

Purification:
  Place a small amount of sage or sweet grass in a bowl and light it with a match. Blow out the flame. Gently blow (breath of life) on the embers to enhance the smoke.
  Using the large feather, fan the smoke around the body of the person sitting next to you in the group.

Introduction:
Raw ingredients of the simmering stew
Placed in a cauldron of suppression.
Heat and time join elements of pressure,
While the lid is in place
No one has to know what is cooking within
Until the lid is blown high into the air
Because no one heeded the signs of steam.

  The people of the Hawaiian Islands offered sacrifices to the goddess Pele to avoid invoking her wrath. When Pele becomes angry, Mt. Kilauea erupts, and the lava causes the destruction of everything in its path. Stored anger tends to erupt like a volcano. Instead of an energy, which directly confronts a particular person or situation, the volcanic discharge of rage destroys what is close at hand.

Ceremony:
  As the ceremonial leader begins to light the candles, each member of the ceremony stands up and stretches. Each person will require his or her own space with which to work this ceremony. There will be a great deal of energy to discharge, and each person must release this energy in their own space in order not to violate another member of the group.
  The leader of the ceremony begins to drum quietly. Others in the group pick up drums and rattles. They join in the rhythm. When everyone is participating in the pulsation, the leader raises the intensity of drumming. As the rhythm grows louder and faster, some members of the group may begin to pace as they drum, others might find themselves vocalizing their energy. At the peak of

the ceremony movement may turn to swaying, stomping, or jumping up and down. Vocalizing may turn to cursing, yelling, screaming, or animal-like noises.

Upon a signal from the ceremonial leader, the drumming energy begins to quiet down. The rhythm is slower and more unified. Eventually the rhythm slows down to that of a heart beat, and then fades to quiet.

When the participants have quieted down, have each one speak about the experience of releasing the anger and rage, and how they might find ways not to let these feelings build up in the future.

Closing:

Thank and release the spirits for attending the ritual. Have everyone mark the forehead of the person next to them with Ylang-ylang oil. Say the words, "remember the volcanic fires of Pele."

Honoring Our Vessel

The heat of summer exposes the vessel of our being. What have we done with it so far? Do we eat well? Do we nourish ourselves physically? Spiritually? Emotionally? How do we adorn our body? Do we reflect an inner love or beg for outer acceptance? Do we over-indulge in outer aspects to make up for an internal lack? Today we will honor the vessel of our spirit as the vehicle by which our spirit chooses to navigate upon this earth.

Preparation:
1. Wear loose, comfortable clothing.
2. Have people bring their own hairbrushes.
3. Prepare a sacred space for the ceremony.

Materials:
Sage or sweet grass, bowl, and feather
Four body essentials for the four directions (i.e. food, water, love, spirit)
Mirrors
Massage oils
Rose and orange water
Towels
Henna or body paints
Calming music
Timer

Invocation:
We invite to this circle the elements essential to our body.
We invite the spirit of food, of all growing things, whose energy we take into our body to fuel our movement.
We invite the spirit of water, of the refreshing journey that water has taken, from mountain to sea to air and back to earth. We invite the moisture that keeps our bodies from becoming dry.
We invite the spirit of pure love, without which our lives would have no meaning.
We invite the spiritual aspects of life, the spirit within and

the deity of our beliefs. We invite that which encompasses all things.

Purification:

Place a small amount of sage or sweet grass in a bowl and light it with a match. Blow out the flame. Gently blow (breath of life) on the embers to enhance the smoke. Using the large feather, fan the smoke around the body of the person sitting next to you in the group. Fan the smoke over all of the materials to be used in the ritual.

Introduction:

Hands received my being
When I entered into this world.
Sing the story of my body,
Undo the false teachings
Remove the inappropriate
From this vessel.
Let my skin rejoice!!

Ceremony:

The body is a sacred thing. When we work together with each other to honor and respect ourselves, we must remember to honor and respect each other's boundaries. Permission must be given in order to enter one another's sacred space. A quiet trust-building region must be established before we begin each aspect of the ceremony. Ask for permission and *wait* for the other person to give it. The person giving permission must *wait* until they are ready to truly give their permission.

Note: People can work in small groups or pairs. Different activities may be substituted for the ones suggested here. The first and last activity everyone can do within the group.

Face Staring. Set a timer for two minutes. Have each person look into a mirror. Have everyone notice the shape of their own face; the color of their eyes, the feel of their skin, their teeth, lips, eyelashes, etc. Some people may express embarrassment by giggling, some may cry. Remind everyone to breathe deeply and focus on his or her face. When the two minutes are up. Have everyone say "I love you" to themselves in the mirror.

Foot bath. Ask permission, "may I have permission to give you a foot bath? I promise to honor your boundaries." Wait for the answer. Anointing the feet of another person is an ancient ritual of love and respect. Gently rub the foot with rose and orange water. You are honoring the vehicle of movement, the metaphor of progression. Remove the tension and stress caused by seeking perfection. Bless the feet as you wash them. Anoint them with oil. Gently dry them when you are done.

Upper back massage. Ask permission, "may I have permission to give you an upper back massage? I promise to honor your boundaries." Wait for the answer. The weight of the world is said to be carried on our shoulders. Unexpressed feelings harbor themselves in our upper back as we constantly brace ourselves for each experience in life. Loosen the upper back from the burdens it carries. Bless the upper back with caresses as well as massage.

Hand Massage. Ask permission, "may I have permission to give your hands a massage? I promise to honor your boundaries." Wait for the answer. The hands speak the language of the soul. Touch implies intimacy. Touch gathers information. Touch connects. Hands hold, hurt, manipulate, maneuver, and speak to those who cannot hear and to those who can. As you massage the hands, remove all cramping fear; unfold the clenching of control. Massage each finger as if it were an entity unto itself. Honor the thumb that separates us from other fingered animals. Honor the many facets of movement on each finger.

Hair brushing. Ask permission, "may I have permission to you an brush your hair? I promise to honor your boundaries." Wait for the answer. If "brushing" is not an option, then running your fingers through the hair and massaging the scalp will work just as well. The crown is the center of connection to the spiritual. Our connection to the universe. A sense of calm can engulf the entire body from closing your eyes and letting another brush your hair. Hair is the artistic expression of the Creator. Each strand is numbered and respected.

Face Staring. Once again, set a timer for two minutes. Have each person look into a mirror. Have everyone notice the shape of their own face; the color of their eyes, the feel of their skin, their teeth, lips, eyelashes, etc. After experiencing the honoring of your body, are your feelings different. Breathe deeply and focus on your face. When the two minutes are up. Have everyone say "I love you" to themselves in the mirror.

Closing:
Release the spirits from the circle. End with hugs and feasting.

September Rituals

Leaving the Nest

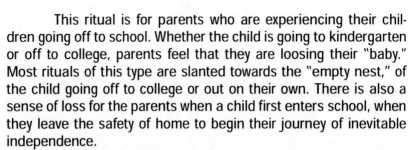

This ritual is for parents who are experiencing their children going off to school. Whether the child is going to kindergarten or off to college, parents feel that they are loosing their "baby." Most rituals of this type are slanted towards the "empty nest," of the child going off to college or out on their own. There is also a sense of loss for the parents when a child first enters school, when they leave the safety of home to begin their journey of inevitable independence.

The ceremonial part of this ritual is broken in two, one for a younger child who is first attending school, and one for a teen going off to college.

Preparation:
1. Select an object of protection that the child can carry when they are away from you - maybe a piece of jewelry, a rock, or a good luck charm.
2. Each family member participating in the ritual is to bring a symbolic object to add to the journey stick.
3. Make the shopping trip for school supplies a special event.

Materials:
Symbol of protection
Favorite color yarn
A stick 3-5 feet tall (walking stick)
Natural (symbolic) objects to place on the stick

Invocation:
Include all members in the offering of a family prayer.

Ceremony:
We are gathered here to honor the start of _____ (child's name) journey to independence.

For the young child who is beginning school

Parents, begin by telling your child the importance of going to school, describe to your child what school was like for you, the special qualities that you have seen in your child and how these qualities could enhance their life when they grow up.

Give your child the symbol of protection for when your are not there. Let your child know that you love them even when you are not with them.

All family members are to help decorate the Journey Stick. Apply the symbolic objects: tie on bells, feathers, colored yarn, beads, paint, etc. When the stick is finished, dedicate the Journey Stick to the beginning of this child's independence.

For the young person going to college
1. To the young person who is going to college, have each family member honor what this person has meant to the family. Share one funny story and one story of love regarding this person.
2. Have the teen that is going away to school share their experience of being a member of the family. Ask them to share what qualities they wish to carry with them when they leave.
3. Loosely wrap the colored yarn between the wrist of parents and child. Cut the yarn to symbolically release the new life of the young person.
4. All family members are to help decorate the Journey Stick. Apply the symbolic objects: tie on bells, feathers, colored yarn, beads, paint, etc. When the stick is finished, dedicate the Journey Stick to the beginning of a new life.

Closing:
Seeds of new life have been planted.
Released from their shells, the young begin to grow.
Embrace one another through the tears of transition.
Soften the earth with release.

Fall Cleaning Ritual

We can elevate the fall cleaning ritual from the chore we have considered it to be, and return this ceremony as a way to consciously prepare our home for the transition of the coming season. Our ancestors prepared their homes for the coming winter by repairing holes, bringing out the warmer blankets, sealing the windows, canning fruits and vegetables, and cutting and stacking firewood. Our sense of survival may not be as dramatic today, but the practice of preparation can make the upcoming winter months a little more enjoyable. You may choose to rearrange furniture, change color schemes, put up storm windows, etc.

Preparation:
1. Find enjoyable music to play in the background while you work.
2. Divide the tasks according to ability, leaving the more difficult tasks as a group effort.
3. Make sure that you have all cleaning and repair supplies on hand.
4. Set an agreeable date for this ritual.

Materials:
Cleaning and repair supplies
Background music
Decorative items (if desired)
Celebration treats (warm cider, cookies, etc.)

Prayer:
The summer is gone.
We must prepare to dwell within.
Bless us as we prepare our home for the coming months.
May every surface be tended to with love.
Let our toil be not a drudgery, but a caress,
An honor to the structure that has sheltered us.

<u>Ceremony</u>:

Autumn winds increase
As nature sweeps the face of our mother clean.
Distinct as a narrator between changing scenes,
The curtain falls at the completion of a season,
Making way for nature's grand finale,
And her encore performance next year.

We gather today to honor the sacred space of our home.

As the body houses the spirit, our homes contain the collection of our souls. For it is here that our memories are born, that our roots have earth beneath them; where every blade of grass remembers our growth, has cradled our daydreams as we have stared into summer skies.

Hand out the task lists, letting each person know that they have the privilege of honoring the home with their ability to complete each job that they are given. Play the background music as you work, sing along if possible. Lift the spirits in your home with your attitude as well as your tasks.

<u>Closing</u>:

Admire the beauty of your home. Delight in the work that has been completed by everyone. Celebrate your collective accomplishment with treats.

October Rituals

Untangling a Web of Deceit

This ritual is to release us from the sticky web of deceit. We have lied. We have been lied to. Those who participate in this ritual must be willing to give up all hope of a better truth, to let go of the fear of being honest with others.

Preparation:

1. Create a "web" by taking an embroidery hoop or some other circular object, and loop string around it, as many times as there will be participants in the ritual. This may require more than one hoop. Dream catcher designs are a great model for creating a ceremonial web of deceit.

2. Have all participants bring "proof" of a lie. One that has been told to them and one that they have told. The "proof" can be symbolic or actual (birth certificate, phone bill, credit card receipt, pictures, descriptions, etc.)

3. All participants are to wear something (visibly) blue.

4. Fill the room with the scent of cedar, sage, or sandalwood.

Materials:
Prepared web
String, knife or scissors
Blue candles
Cedar - purifier, represents honor
Cinnamon oil - draws forth the true will, represents fire
A drum or drum music

Introduction:

At the start of all deceit is the web of attachment, the connecting point where the web began. All lies are a recreation of the world as it presents itself, in order to live the truth of a self-serving fantasy world. On the other end of the lie, the world does not seem as real, perception is pitted against perception until the most convincing view wins.

An intricate web is strung
Delicate yet strong,
Invisible but for the morning dew,
Adding sparkle and luster to a trap of doom.

Patiently, as if she did not exist,
Anticipating the tremble of unsuspecting legs,
The spider waits.

Translucent threads hold fast
To the squirm and struggle
Sending a signal of succulence.
Oh, the fear...
How delicious it will taste.

Invocation:

Fire - We call to this circle, the element of fire. We ask for the purification of the refiners' fire. In this circle, burn away all that is not pure, all that is not true. Leave us with the finest elements of ourselves.

Air - We call to this circle, the element of air. The soaring bird of freedom stretches a vast blue wingspan. Released from the weight of deception, the bird of freedom is at liberty to fly wherever it may.

Earth - We call to this circle, the element of earth. In your dark arms, leech away the poisons of deceit. Restore us to the innocent seed of potential, from the transformed compost of waste.

Water - We call to this circle, the element of water. Bath us in your introspection. Remove from our surface the accumulation of pollutants and refresh us with soft, flowing movement.

Purification:

Rub a drop of cinnamon oil on the throat of the person sitting next to you. Repeat the words "May the truth be released through you."

Ceremony:

Release all other light from the room except for the light of the blue candles. Begin drumming.

Close your eyes. Breathe in and out. With every exhalation, let go of fear, tension and stress. With every inhalation, breathe in the love of the universe. Relax your body. Feel yourself touching the floor. Let go.

As you relax, you begin to feel a slight breeze. A large bird is flying overhead. As the bird circles closer a wind begins to pick up. Looking into this wind, you see a web moving with the air current. Notice what it is attached to. Become aware of how sticky it is, and what it is made of. Look at the delicate, intricate design. Something lures you even though you know the danger.

Before you touch the web, your guide arrives. This guide is dressed in brilliant, almost blinding white. Your guide shows you the truth behind the web, the struggle to mask the pain, the events as they really occurred. As the truth resonates in its fullness, the sound of the drum grows louder. The pain is no longer devastating, true perception fills your body with strength. The vibration of truth begins to release the web from whatever it was attached to. A brilliant blue light emanates from your body. You realize that you have become that soaring bird.

When you are ready, feel your body on the floor, feel your breath flowing in and out, and open your eyes. One at a time, share your experience of the guided meditation with the group.

Closing:
Each participant is to share his or her "proof" of deception. After they have shared what it is or what it represents, they will cut one loop of attachment on the symbolic web of deceit and say these words: "The truth is released, my soul is free."

Claiming Power Ceremony

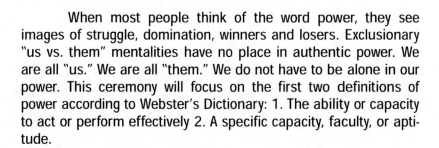

When most people think of the word power, they see images of struggle, domination, winners and losers. Exclusionary "us vs. them" mentalities have no place in authentic power. We are all "us." We are all "them." We do not have to be alone in our power. This ceremony will focus on the first two definitions of power according to Webster's Dictionary: 1. The ability or capacity to act or perform effectively 2. A specific capacity, faculty, or aptitude.

Materials:
Sage or sweet grass
Large feather
Drum or drum music
Candles: yellow, red, black, and white

Invocation:
Light the red candle.
We call to this circle the direction of South. Here we sit in innocence, open to receive the blessings of fulfillment. In the South we are trusting.

Light the yellow candle.
We call to this circle the direction of East, direction of beginnings and illumination. We open our heart to the teachings of this ceremony. In the East we are humble.

Light the black candle.
We call to this circle the direction of West, direction of the evening and introspection. We open our dreams to the knowledge of power, so close, but not yet attainable. In the West we contemplate our learning.

Light the white candle.
We call to this circle the direction of North. Here we sit as the wind carries our prayers; we feel the strength of the ancestors. In the North we release our fears.

Purification:

Place a small amount of sage or sweet grass in a bowl and light it with a match. Blow out the flame. Gently blow (breath of life) on the embers to enhance the smoke.

Using the large feather, fan the smoke around the body of the person sitting next to you in the circle.

Ceremony:

Power, your name has been used in vain
For the whim of human kind.
Like atoms turned to explosives
We cannot stand side by side
In our full potential
Lest we combine into elements
Of destruction.

Release all other light from the room except for the light of the four candles.

Close your eyes. Breathe in and out. With every exhalation, let go of fear, tension and stress. With every inhalation, breathe in the love of the universe. Relax your body. Feel yourself touching the floor. Let go.

Imagine yourself walking. Your destination is your favorite place in the forest. There is a clearing where a group of people have gathered. A bonfire has been lit. Members of the group warm themselves by the fire. They invite you to join them. The feeling is so peaceful that you do not question their motives. You know that you are safe.

You notice an area in the clearing that is filled with gifts. Their content is hidden, but there is one gift that is calling specially to you. A drummer begins to play a tribal beat. It is mesmerizing.

You are asked to choose two members of the group, one to stand on either side of you. You receive this gift. You are told that it is a gift of power, but that you cannot open it alone. Those on either side of you

must open it with you. No one of the three of you can hold back. No one of the three of you can take the lead.

What is your gift?

Now you are asked to give away your fear of utilizing this

gift. You must turn it into a shape and cast it into the fire. Once again, you must not undertake this task alone. Once again, those on either side of you must assist. No one of the three of you can hold back. No one of the three of you can take the lead.

What did you give away? What shape was it?

The fire burns higher. All of the members of the group begin to dance. Their shouts fill the clearing in the forest as they all celebrate your gift. They have gifts as well.

The group bids you farewell as you leave the forest clearing. The tribal drums begin to fade.

When you are ready, feel your body on the floor, feel your breath flowing in and out, and open your eyes. One at a time, share your experience of the guided meditation with the group.

<u>Closing</u>:

Release the spirit of the directions. Thank the spirits for attending the group.

November Rituals

Releasing Isolation

This ritual is a gift, for those who participate, given to those who have not released the chilling agony of isolation. It is a healing for all that are involved. Resistance may be felt to the process of becoming fully open. Everyone must cooperate in assisting one another in their moments of holding back, for this is a ritual of rebirth into the self that was originally meant to be.

Materials:
Safe individuals
A quiet outdoor setting, preferably the woods

In a disorganized pile place the following:
   A large, heavy rock
   A sharp object: piece of glass or knife
   Autumn leaves
   Four pieces of wood
   Dried (brittle) twigs or small branches

Introduction:
   Today we are going to release the bonds of isolation and join together the hearts of one among many.

One more instance of being the odd one out.
One more time, the body language has said
We two do not wish to be interrupted by you.
Silently walking away has not worked.
Fighting for the right of her place has not worked.
Turning herself into what they wished has not worked -
Has left her empty
Less likely than ever
To finally belong...
She cannot bury this altar identity,
It would not honor the service it has provided.
She cannot do this alone...

There are a few, who have volunteered,

Ignored her cries to be left alone,
With these people backing her
She begins a ritual of letting go,
Lying to rest the armor, blockades and false selves,
Letting go to accepting love.

Invocation/Purification:

Everyone is to join hands, close their eyes, and spend a moment in silence (at least 30 seconds) to draw energy from the center of their bodies.

With hands joined and eyes closed, the officiator will offer a spiritual prayer for the alliance and courage required to complete this ritual.

When the prayer has been completed, each participant will ask out loud for Spirit to remove all fear from his or her thinking.

Ceremony:

The one in need of healing has some work to do. This work must be done in the midst of the willingness to trust others. Words are not to be spoken except by anyone except by the officiator to the one in need of healing. Trusting the support of others is a key part of this ritual. The one in need of healing must re-learn to hear love in all of its quiet forms.

Officiator: Remove the heavy rock from the pile of materials and place it in the center of our circle. Repeat the words "I place into this center of love, the hardness and heaviness of my load."

The one to be healed: "I place into this center of love, the hardness and heaviness of my load."

Officiator: Remove the sharp object from the pile of materials and place it next to the rock in the center of our circle. Repeat the words " I place into this center of love, the barbs I have used to keep others at a distance."

The one to be healed: " I place into this center of love, the barbs I have used to keep others at a distance."

Officiator: Remove the brilliant autumn leaves from the pile of materials and place it next to the sharp object in the center of our circle. Place it in such a way to form a circle with an empty center. Repeat the words " I place into this center of love, the short-lived costumes from the roles of my life."

The one to be healed: " I place into this center of love, the short-lived costumes from the roles of my life."

Officiator: Remove the four pieces of wood from the pile of materials and place them in a square next to the brilliant autumn leaves. Repeat the words " I place into this center of love, the walls I have used to keep others out."

The one to be healed: " I place into this center of love the walls I have used to keep others out."

Officiator: Remove the dried twigs from the remaining pile and place them next to the four pieces of wood. Repeat the words " I place into the center of love, the dried, fragile self I have become."

The one to be healed: " I place into the center of love, the dried, fragile self I have become."

Officiator: Feel your emptiness. Pull all of the empty feelings from within your body and your thinking. Bring the emptiness into your hands. Place your emptiness in the center of the other materials. Repeat the words " I place into the center of love, in the center of all of my symbols of isolation, the agony of my emptiness."

The one to be healed: " I place into the center of love, in the center of all of my symbols of isolation, the agony of my emptiness."

Officiator: Look at your symbolic isolation. See the heavy burden of hardness, the barbed defenses, the costumes of false selves, the walls of isolation, the fragile, shattered self, and the nothingness of being so alone. Repeat the words " Within the center of love, I lay to rest these symbols of isolation. I turn to you who are willing to support me, as symbols of hope."

The one to be healed: " Within the center of love, I lay to rest these symbols of isolation. I turn to you who are willing to support me, as symbols of hope."

<u>Closing</u>: At this time, the supporting members of the ritual may demonstrate to the one in need of healing, silent evidences of love (gently wipe away tears, calmly caress, hold, etc.).

Ritual of Abundance

Warning: rituals of abundance often require the partici-pants to examine a mentality of lack. If you officiate this ritual, you will have to take a close look at these issues.

This ritual was performed for a group of women. It can be modified to include men as well.

Materials:
Candle (deep red or gold) - East. Soil - South
Water - West. Incense - North
Stalks of wheat for purification.

Introduction:
Welcome to November. Evening of the year.
Sunshine fades as clocks have changed,
Re-arranging the length of our known days.
Leaves display an intensity of color
Before they dry and fade to the ground.
November winds carry secret messages through the dark woods,
Breeding stories of fantastic proportions.
Brilliant colors of leaf and harvest adorn our homes:
Reds and gold's, oranges, and browns.
The world begins a retreat within.
Family begins to gather.
It is a time of abundance, harvest and gratitude.

After the toil of planting seed
The fending off of weed, heat and predator,
Of gathering harvest and the preparations to store,
Comes a restless moment in Puritan work,
Of rest, blessing and abundance.
The question of, is there enough to last
Is never asked by those who gather,
Only the question of where that matters.
A pause to celebrate the harvest brought in
Before the pattern is repeated
And the next cycle begins.

Invocation:
West
We call to this circle the Western direction,
The season of autumn,
Sun setting into the horizon above the water.
We call into this circle
Your spirit of introspection.
East
We call to this circle the direction of East,
The beginning from whence we came.
We remember your bright sunlight awakening our days.
We call into this circle
Your spirit of wisdom.
South
We call to this circle the Southern direction,
The earthly foundation of our grounding,
Remembering the recent passing of summer.
We call into this circle
Your spirit of trust.
North
We call to this circle the direction of North,
Accepting the underground journey of winter.
In the winds of the north our prayers are carried.
We call into this circle
Your spirit of strength.

Purification
As we go around the circle, purify the woman beside you
with the stalk of wheat and these words:
You are a goddess of abundance

GUIDED MEDITATION - Journey of Abundance
1. Gathering of Light
2. Preparing a Space
3. Belief in the Seed
4. Defending Growth
5. Gathering the Harvest
6. Celebration

Gathering of Light
From November's soft warm cloak of darkness
The radiant inner fire of women's authenticity
Sheds a solitary ray of light.
Light by light we gather together,
As brilliant as the summer sun.
Close your eyes and feel the warmth of your glow.
Find the one word that is the light of your authenticity.

Preparing a Space
Preparing a space is a remembering or a beginning.
There is a landscape before the clearing,
The woods before a cottage is built,
An overgrown field before crops are planted,
Relationships of pain before the coming of joy.
What preparation is required for your space?

Belief in the Seed
In the package is a seed.
In brilliant color, temperature zones are divided
With times of planting, depth and spacing.
Requirements of warmth and water,
Pruning and gathering, height, and sizes -
All faith in the potential of a seed.
What must you believe as you plant your first seed?

Defending Growth
Long ago I made a pact
For the seeds I planted not to grow.
In the world of seed, the enemies
Are weed, flood, drought, insects,
Grazing animals and neglect.
The seeds I plant are doomed,
Lest I defend against doubt, fear
Ignorance, isolation, giving up,
Sabotage and neglect.
What pact did you make to hinder the growth of your seeds?

Gathering the Harvest
Apples fall from the trees, but not into my home.
All around me, abundance is available.
My basket is large.
I may fill it as many times as I wish.
I know how to preserve and cure.
I gather the abundance.
I have more than enough.
I have cause for celebration.
What abundance have you harvested?
What tools were used for harvest?
How big is your basket? How many times have you filled it?

Celebration
I have cause for celebration.
I choose to celebrate with you.
I bring my share of abundance to the table,
In gratitude and thanksgiving.

When you are ready, open your eyes.
We will go around the circle and share our journey of abundance.

December Rituals

Ritual to Honor Darkness

---◆---

*"Mere suppression of the shadow is as little
of a remedy as beheading would be for a headache."*

-Carl Jung

During this season, darkness has swallowed a greater portion of our days. The shadow has lived in repression for 6 months of the year and now it returns to lay claim to its importance in life. In the dark corners of our world, we hide what we cannot discard; we push aside excesses, labeling them as "too much." And yet, if the sun were to shine all day, we would surely wither and die.

We must not fear the darkness anymore than we would fear the light. Black is the color associated with mastery. White signifies the pure beginning while black signifies the collective ending. Those who have mastered certain skills in the martial arts achieve a black belt. Without darkness, the light has no definition.

Preparation:

1. Request that all participants in the ritual are to wear something dark. They do not have to wear "black" in particular, but some shade of dark color.

2. Think about "dark" qualities, that which is frowned upon, or not considered to be proper. Write one of these qualities on an index card.

3. During the ritual, these "dark qualities" are going to be "internalized." Cut enough apples for each participant to eat a slice.

4. Darken the room where the ritual will be held. Have only candlelight when the participants enter the place of ritual. Purification happens in the candle light or outside of the darkened ritual area.

5. Burn incense to purify the ritual space. Quiet drumming or drumming music may be used to accompany the procession into the shadows.

Materials:
Apples
Index cards
Decorations: glue, crayons, pens, ribbons, glitter, stickers, etc.
Candles: black and red
Bowl of salt water
Owl feathers or other objects symbolizing the night
Incense
Drum or drum music

Purification:
      Each participant begins by dipping his or her finger in the bowl of salt water. Have the participant touch the forehead of the person sitting next to them and say the words, "You have permission to release what is trapped in the shadows."

Invocation:
      We call to this circle the direction of East, the place of new beginnings, dawn, and the winged ones. We call the spirits of the East to bring us the freedom to be our authentic selves.
      We call to this circle the direction of South, the place where fire burns with passion, place of the midday sun and emotional intensity. We call the spirits of the South to touch us with wildness, with passion and sensuality.
      We call to this circle the direction of West, the place of the sun setting below the horizon, the place of night, and of introspection. We call the spirits of the West to guide us as we journey through our inner caverns of darkness.
      We call to this circle the direction of North, the place of winter, the place of ancient ancestors. We call the spirits of the North to teach us of the secret jewel buried in our shadows.

Introduction:

A shadow in the dark.
A shadow in the dark cannot be seen,
But the shadow knows itself,
Knows it exists,
Even as shadow
In the dark.

We gather today to honor the lessons of darkness. We have condemned to the unconscious that which we do not wish to acknowledge. The light must define what is hidden in the shadows. That which is hidden in the light must be defined by the dark. In this world, there cannot be one without the other.

Ceremony:

Ask all participants to blow out their candles. The officiator may keep their candle lit, if necessary, in order to read. Begin a soft beat on the drum - a heartbeat, a focusing point.

Close your eyes. Breathe in and out. With every exhalation, let go of fear, tension and stress. With every inhalation, breathe in the love of the universe. Relax your body. Focus on the sound of the drum. Feel yourself touching the floor. Let go.

As you become more and more relaxed, you begin to see yourself in your favorite, free, open space. You may see yourself playing in an open field, dancing with arms spread wide along the shore of the ocean, or laying back against the comfort of your favorite tree. The sun shines upon your face. You drink in the warmth through every pore of your body. While playing in this free space, you notice a place where there is a dark entrance. Maybe it is the entrance to a cave, a hole in a large tree, or the secret entrance to an underground cavern. (If you are too frightened to enter this dark place alone, ask for the assistance of a guide to accompany you on this adventure).

As you enter this dark space, you notice light fading. As you feel your way through the darkness, take note of the space you are in. Is it closed and confining, musty smelling, are you comfortable here, does it have rough walls, is the temperature cold or warm? Your eyes are becoming accustomed to the dark. What you could only perceive with your hands now becomes visible. There is still no actual "light," but your being has illuminated your senses. You find something in this dark place - a gift has been left especially for you. As you take it in your hands you find an aspect of yourself that had been banished. You find that this aspect is covered with judgment and humiliation. When you clean the debris from the aspect, it becomes a jewel that begins to glow. The glow fills the dark cavern with a warm light. The entrance to the cavern is illuminated. You find your way out and travel back to the open place where you began.

When you are ready, feel your body on the floor, feel your breath flowing in and out, and open your eyes. One at a time, share the experience of your guided meditation with the group.

When we honor dark aspects of ourselves we begin to have choice. With choice, we have the freedom to live our lives without secrets and without harming others. We will not surprise ourselves with actions we regret later.

To honor our dark aspects, we will now decorate our "dark aspects" index cards.

Closing:

Before the first apple was eaten, the world was already divided into both day and night. We came to know both "good" and "evil" and wanted to have ourselves identified as the actor of one or the other. Today, we eat a slice of apple to signify our choices without fear. We take within ourselves the dark aspects without loathing. Say the words; "I no longer fear my_____(dark aspect).

Thank and release the spirits for attending the ritual. Celebrate with feasting.

Setting-Free Ritual

*And in the corners accumulated among dustballs,
exhaled by those who have entered here, the desires.
Of all things in my store, they are the most ancient.*

-The Mistress of Spices

The discomfort that comes from holding on too long causes the body to ache. The mind becomes driven by a longing for something yet unnamed. The desire must be set free. Painful feelings must be soothed. Sorrows must be released.

This ritual is short but powerful. It can be performed alone or in the company of others. The purpose is to release that which has been trapped within.

Preparation:

1.Focus on the person, place or thing that you need to set free.

2.Ask yourself, what fears am I willing to shed? What repressed feelings or painful memories am I willing to let go of?

3.Create a sacred space. Make sure that it is a quiet place where you will not be disturbed. Decorate it with vibrant red colors.

4.Determine a safe place for burning paper.

Materials:
Pencil and paper
Sage or sweet grass
Large feather
"Medicine" blanket (a blanket of comfort)
4 White candles

Purification:

Place a small amount of sage or sweet grass in a bowl and light it with a match. Blow out the flame. Gently blow (breath of life) on the embers to enhance the smoke. Using the large feather, fan the smoke around your body (solitary ritual) or around the body of

174

the person sitting next to you in the group. Fan the smoke over all materials to be used during the ritual. Spread out your medicine blanket in the midst of the sacred circle. Remember that your blanket creates a shield of safety through comfort.

Invocation:
Light the 4 white candles as you call each direction to the circle.

> We call to this circle the direction of West. We ask that our meditation and our dreaming bring that which has been held so long.
> We call to this circle the direction of South. We ask the earth to cradle our bodies in safety, like that of an innocent child.
> We call to this circle the direction of East. We ask for the wisdom of fire to carry our thoughts and feelings to the air for release.
> We call to this circle the direction of North. We ask for the air to carry our freed feelings to a place of healing.

Ceremony:
As the body contains carbon, so does the lead of a pencil. With pencil and paper, we will remove from our bodies and our minds, disappointments, despair, and painful emotions.

Write down on the paper the person place or thing that needs to be released. Write down all associated feelings, fears, memories, and belief systems. When you feel that you have cleaned out all that you possibly can take the paper and burn it. As the smoke and flames reach into the air say, I release this_____. Ask the smoke to carry your pain away, ask the air to cleanse it. It is important to ask for your body and soul to become filled with peace and serenity, to fill the emptiness created by removing the negative feelings.

Closing:
Thank and release the elements from the circle. Spend some quiet time of reflection.

Closing

Closing

———————< ◆ >———————

Enter the search word "ritual" on an internet search engine and you will be directed to a multitude of listings, anywhere from satanic ritual abuse to religious family bonding. Our modern social and family living standards have abandoned or de-emphasized many of the once common social and ceremonial processes. At the same time, the stress and anxiety of major life changes still occur on a daily basis. The practise of ritual ceremonies exerts powerful energy for making these life changes easier.

If the practise of ritual is so powerful and effective then why are we no longer including rituals in our lives? The answer may be that we have not abandoned the concept of ritual entirely, but that as a society, we are searching for rituals that contain more meaning. The following excerpt, from the essay *Rituals and Modern Society* by Serge Kahili King, illustrates this point.

"Many of modern society's rituals have lost their satisfaction because their performance is not as effective as it used to be, and because new issues important to people are not being addressed by those traditionally looked to for meaningful rituals. The purposed of a ritual is to impress and influence people, but too many of society's standard rituals are being done for the sake of tradition or dogma or habit alone and those who are leading them are no longer impressed or influenced by them. So people are increasingly seeking out different rituals to meet their needs for significance and enjoyment. This is one reason why such large numbers of people are now interested in shamanism, which includes dance, song, touch, and connections with Nature, as well as joy, meaning and creativity in its rituals. As the people of the world continue to grow in love and confidence they will have more freedom to adapt ancient rituals for modern use, rejuvenate the dead ones of the present society, or create entirely new ones at will. This is exactly what is happening now, and it's a very good sign for the future."39

[39.]King, Serge *Rituals and Modern Society*

Suggested Reading

Arnold, Charles *Ritual Body Art - Drawing the Spirit*. Custer, Washington: Phoenix Publishing Inc., 1997

Arrien, Angeles *The Four-Fold Way*. San Francisco, California: HarperSanFrancisco, 1993

Blackwolf, and Jones, Gina *Earth Dance Drum: A Celebration of Life*. Salt Lake City, Utah: Commune-A-Key Publishing, 1996

Blair, Nancy *Amulets of the Goddess*. Oakland, California: Wingbow Press, 1993

Breathnach, Sarah Ban *Simple Abundance: A Daybooks of Comfort and Joy*. New York, New York: Warner Books, 1995

Carnes, Robin Deen and Craig, Sally *Sacred Circles: A Guide to Creating Your Own Women's Spirituality Group*. San Francisco, California: HarperSanFrancisco, 1998

Cornell, Judith PH.D *Mandala: Luminous Symbols for Healing*. Wheaton, Illinois: Quest Books, 1994

Cosman, Madeleine Pelner *Medieval Holidays and Festivals*. New York, New York: Charles Scribner's Sons, 1981

Cowan, Tom *Shamanism as a Spiritual Practice for Daily Life*. Freedom, California: The Crossing Press, 1996

Fincher, Susanne F. *Creating Mandalas*. Boston, Massachusetts: Shambala Publications, Inc., 1991

Lake-Thom, Bobby *Spirits of the Earth*. New York, New York: Plume, 1997

L'Engle, Madeleine, *A Wind in the Door*. New York, New York: Farrar, Straus & Giroux, 1973

Louden, Jennifer *The Woman's Retreat Book*. San Francisco, California: HarperSanFrancisco, 1997

Lysne, Robin Heerens *Dancing Up the Moon*. Berkeley, California: Conari Press, 1995

Moondance, Wolf *Spirit Medicine*. New York, New York: Sterling Publishing Co., Inc., 1995

Moore, Thomas *Care of the Soul*. New York, New York: HarperCollins Publishers, Inc., 1992

SARK. *Inspiration Sandwich*. Berkeley, California: Celestial Arts, 1992

Some, Malidoma Patrice *Ritual: Power, Healing and Community*. Portland, Oregon: Swan/Raven & Company, 1993

Starck, Marcia & Stern, Gynne *The Dark Goddess - Dancing With the Shadow*. Freedom, California: The Crossing Press, 1993

Wilson, Sule Greg *The Drummer's Path*. Rochester, Vermont: Destiny Books, 1992

Bibliography

Arguelles, Jose & Miriam *Mandala*. Boston, Massachusetts: Shambhala Publications, Inc., 1972

Arnold, Charles *Ritual Body Art - Drawing the Spirit*. Custer, Washington: Phoenix Publishing Inc., 1997

Arrien, Angeles *The Four-Fold Way*. San Francisco, California: HarperSanFrancisco, 1993

Atwood, Mary Dean *Spirit Healing - Native American Magic & Medicine*

Cornell, Judith *Mandala*. Wheaton, Illinois: Quest Books, 1994

Cosman, Madeleine Pelner *Medieval Holidays and Festivals*. New York, New York: Charles Scribner's Sons, 1981

Cowan, Tom *Shamanism as a Spiritual Practice for Daily Life*. Freedom, California: The Crossing Press, 1996

Cunningham, Nancy Brady *I am Woman by Rite*. York Beach, Maine: Samuel Weiser, Inc., 1995

Duerk, Judith *I Sit Listening to the Wind*. San Diego, California: LuraMedia, 1993

Eagle Man, Ed McGaa *Mother Earth Spirituality*

Fergusson, Erna *Dancing Gods: Indian Ceremonials of New Mexico and Arizona*. Albuquerque, New Mexico: University of New Mexico Press, 1988

Fincher, Susanne F. *Creating Mandalas*. Boston, Massachusetts: Shambala Publications, Inc., 1991

Hart, Mickey & Lieberman, Fredric *Planet Drum*. San Francisco, California: HarperSanFrancisco, 1991

Ingpen, Robert & Wilkinson, Phillip *A Celebration of Customs & Rituals of the World*

King, Serge Kahili *Rituals and Modern Society*. Kilauea, Hawaii: Aloha International, 1997

Lake-Thom, Bobby *Spirits of the Earth*. New York, New York: Plume, 1997

L'Engle, Madeleine, *A Wind in the Door*. New York, New York: Farrar, Straus & Giroux, 1973

Moore, Thomas *Care of the Soul*. New York, New York: HarperCollins Publishers, Inc., 1992

Oesterley, W.O.E. *The Sacred Dance*. Brooklyn, New York: Dance Horizons, Inc., 1923

Roth, Gabrielle, with John Loudon *Maps to Ecstasy: Teachings of an Urban Shaman*. San Rafael, California: New World Library, 1989

Sachs, Curt *World History of the Dance*. New York, New York: W.W. Norton & Company, Inc., 1937

Some, Malidoma Patrice *Ritual: Power, Healing and Community*. Portland, Oregon: Swan/Raven & Company, 1993

Starck, Marcia *Women's Medicine Ways*. Freedom, California The Crossing Press, 1993

Starck, Marcia & Stern, Gynne *The Dark Goddess - Dancing With the Shadow*. Freedom, California: The Crossing Press, 1993

Stein, Diane *Casting the Circle, A Women's Book of Ritual*. Freedom, California: The Crossing Press, 1990

Stein, Diane *The Women's Spirituality Book*. St. Paul, Minnesota: Llewellyn Publications, 1995

Vlahos, Olivia *Body, The Ultimate Symbol, Meanings of the Human Body Through Time and Place*. New York, New York: Lippincott, 1979

Wilson, Sule Greg *The Drummer's Path*. Rochester, Vermont: Destiny Books, 1992

Wolkstein, Diane & Kramer, Samuel Noah *Inanna Queen of Heaven and Earth*. New York, New York: Harper & Row Publishers, 1983

Ywahoo, Dhani *Voices of Our Ancestors*